PREFACE

To be most useful, this Answer Book should be referred to **after** one has done the exercises, or attempted to, in **Elementary Rudiments of Music**. In this way, answers can be verified, and seeing the correct answer can help in understanding the pertinent theoretical musical point.

The answers in this book are, to the best of my knowledge, correct, logical, and straightforward. I have endeavoured to indicate, wherever applicable, instances where alternative answers may legitimately be acceptable. These may sometimes appear at the bottom of the page. The figures in brackets after the word EXERCISES refer to the page numbers in the original text book where these exercises appear.

The mastery of music theory is a necessary skill and one which touches upon all other aspects of music. It is my hope that this book will help to make the study of music theory easier and more understandable.

Dr. John B. Younger
Editor Emeritus
Frederick Harris Music

Canadian Cataloguing in Publication Data

Younger, John B., 1913–
Elementary rudiments answer book

Supplement to: Wharram, Barbara. Elementary rudiments of music.
ISBN 0-88797-193-8

1. Music — Theory, Elementary — Problems, exercises, etc.
I. Wharram, Barbara. Elementary rudiments of music. II. Title.

MT7.W482 1985 781 C85-099778-X

F.H. 8537

PRINTED IN CANADA

A B C EXERCISES (p. 3)

1. Write the following notes in the treble clef.

   a) F on a line
   b) A in a space
   c) G on a line
   d) C in a space
   e) E on a line
   f) F in a space
   g) B on a line
   h) D in a space
   i) G in a space
   j) Middle C

2. Write the following notes in the bass clef.

   a) B in a space
   b) F on a line
   c) Middle C
   d) A on a line
   e) E in a space
   f) D on a line
   g) G in a space
   h) F in a space
   i) G on a line
   j) C in a space

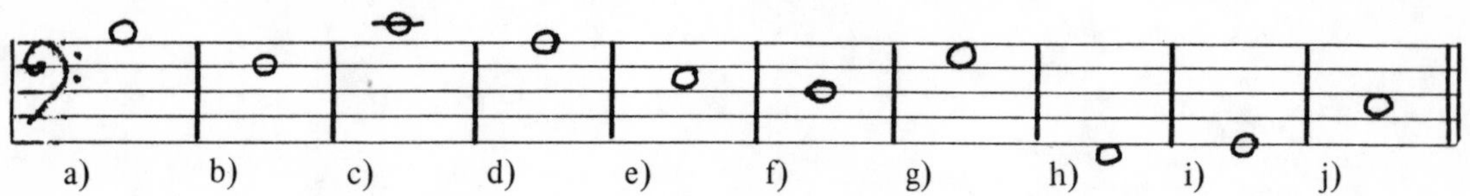

3. Under each of these notes write its letter-name.

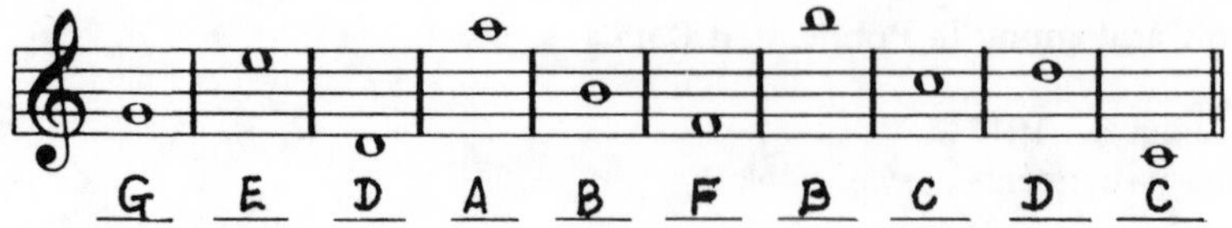

4. Under each of these notes write its letter-name.

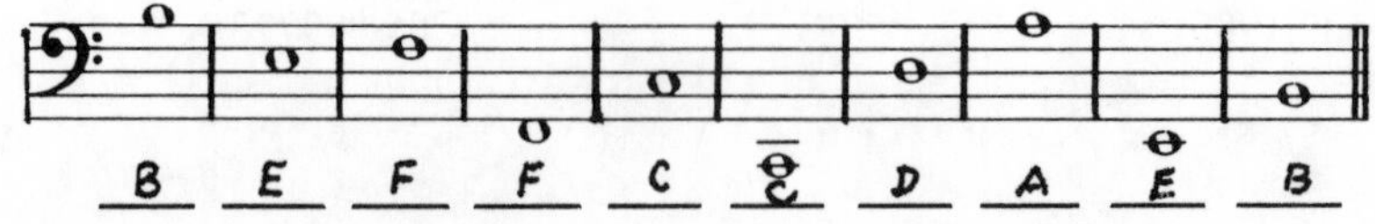

NOTE: If more experience is needed in the naming of notes, the student is advised to practise on sheet music that is readily available to him.

C MORE EXERCISES (p. 4)

1. Under each of these notes write its letter-name.

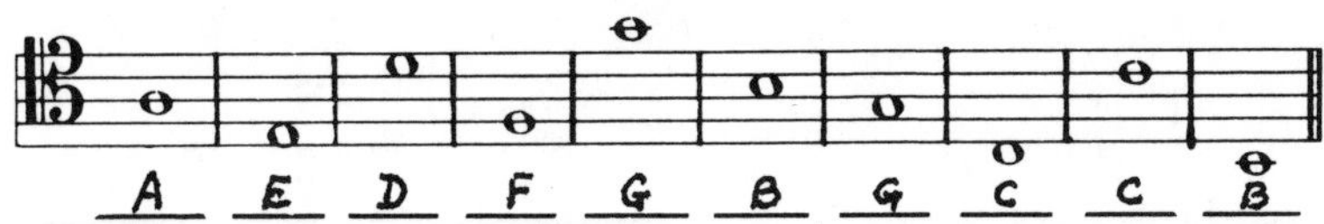

2. Under each of these notes write its letter-name.

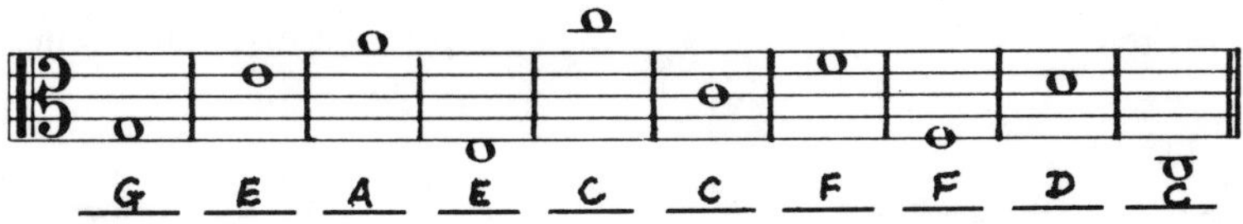

3. Write these notes in the Alto clef.

a) A on a line
b) G on a line
c) D in a space
d) F on a line
e) E in a space
f) B in a space
g) A in a space
h) Middle C
i) G in a space
j) E on a line

4. Write these notes in the tenor clef.

a) D on a line
b) G in a space
c) A on a line
d) E in a space
e) D in a space
f) F on a line
g) Middle C
h) F in a space
i) B in a space
j) E on a line

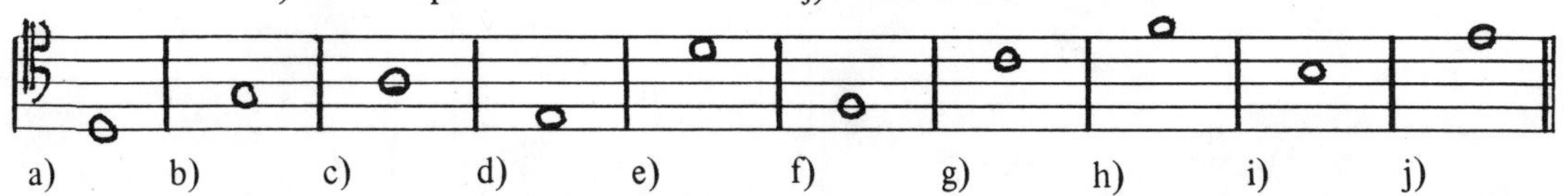

A B C EXERCISES (p. 7)

1. Write ONE note which is equal to the value of each of the following.

a) 

d) =

b) =

e) =

c) =

f) =

2. Write ONE rest which is equal to the value of each of the following.

a) =

f) =

b) =

g) =

c) =

h) =

d) =

i) =

e) =

j) =

3. Write THREE notes which are equal to the value of each of the following.

a) = or

c) = or

b) = or

d) = or

4. Write TWO rests which are equal to the value of each of the following.

a) =

c) =

b) =

d) =

5. Complete the following sentences.

a) 2 quarter notes = 4 eighth notes.

b) 1 half note = 2 quarter notes

c) 3 eighth notes = 6 sixteenth notes

d) 1 quarter note = 4 sixteenth notes

e) 2 eighth notes = 1 quarter note

f) 4 sixteenth notes = 2 eighth notes

g) 2 half notes = 1 whole note

h) 1 whole note = 8 eighth notes

i) 4 thirty-second notes = 2 sixteenth notes

j) 2 sixteenth notes = 1 eighth note

k) A dotted quarter note = 3 eighth notes

l) 3 half notes = a dotted whole note

m) A dotted half note = 6 eighth notes

n) 6 sixteenth notes = 12 thirty-second notes

o) A dotted half note = 3 quarter notes

6. Write a single note (or a dotted note) which is equal to the value of each of the following.

a) = ________

b) = ________

c) = ________

d) = ________

e) = ________

f) = ________

g) = ________

h) = ________

i) = ________

j) = ________

7. Write a single rest (or dotted rest) which is equal to the value of each of the following.

a) =

b) =

c) =

d) =

e) =

f) =

g) =

h) =

8. Write a single note (or dotted note) which is equal to the value of each of the following.

a) =

b) =

c) =

d) =

e) =

f) =

A B C EXERCISES (p. 10)

1. State whether each of the following is a diatonic semitone, a chromatic semitone or a whole tone.

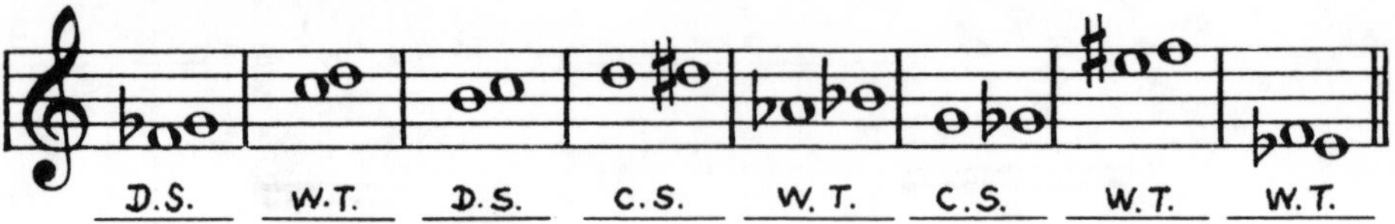

2. Write a chromatic semitone above each of these notes.

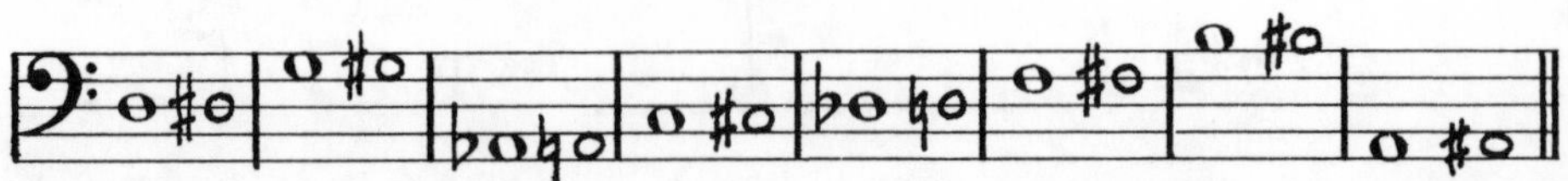

3. Write a diatonic semitone above each of these notes.

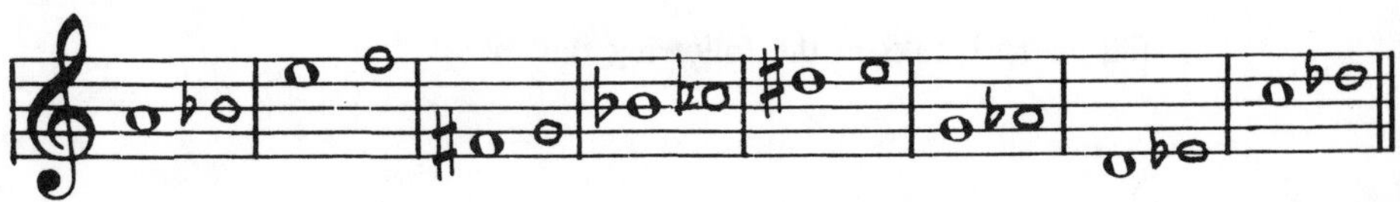

4. Write a chromatic semitone below each of these notes.

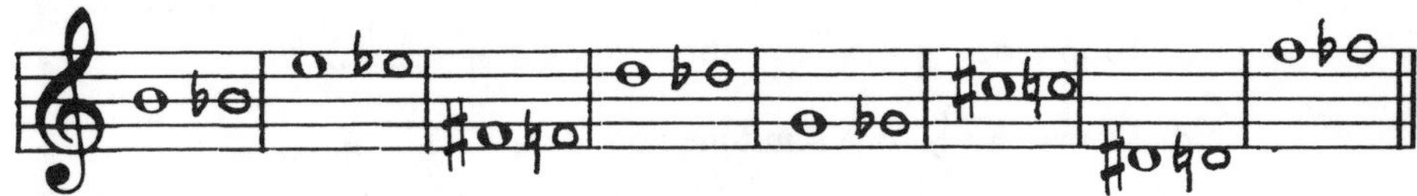

5. Write a diatonic semitone below each of these notes.

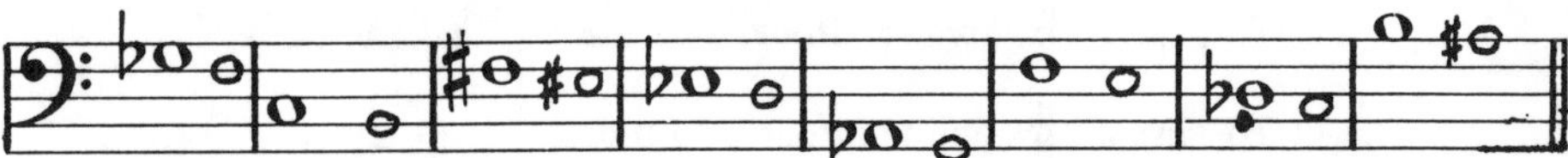

6. Give another name for each of these notes.

a) F♯ G♭ b) B♭ A♯ c) C B♯ d) A♭ G♯ e) F E♯ f) D♯ E♭ g) D♭ C♯

7. Name all the whole tones found between pairs of white keys on the piano.

C–D, D–E, F–G, G–A, A–B

8. Name all the whole tones found between pairs of black keys on the piano.

C♯–D♯, F♯–G♯, G♯–A♯ or D♭–E♭, G♭–A♭, A♭–B♭

9. Write a whole tone above each of these notes.

10. Write a whole tone below each of these notes.

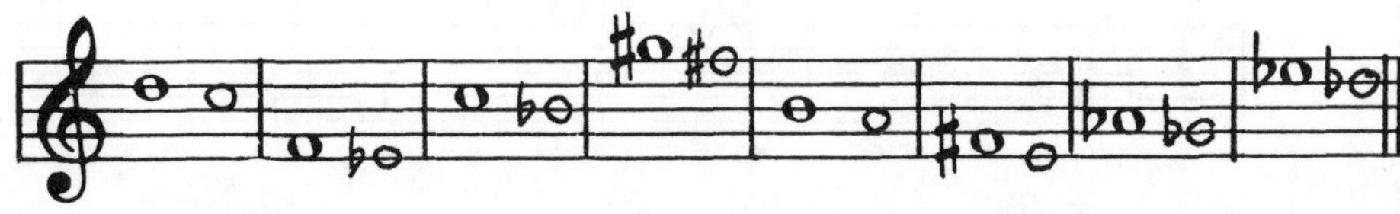

B C MORE EXERCISES (p. 12)

1. Fill in the blanks in the following statements.

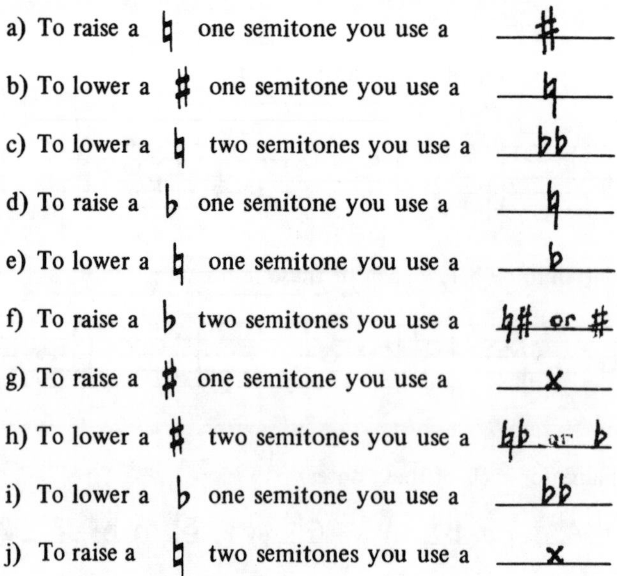

a) To raise a ♮ one semitone you use a ♯

b) To lower a ♯ one semitone you use a ♮

c) To lower a ♮ two semitones you use a ♭♭

d) To raise a ♭ one semitone you use a ♮

e) To lower a ♮ one semitone you use a ♭

f) To raise a ♭ two semitones you use a ♮♯ or ♯

g) To raise a ♯ one semitone you use a x

h) To lower a ♯ two semitones you use a ♮♭ or ♭

i) To lower a ♭ one semitone you use a ♭♭

j) To raise a ♮ two semitones you use a x

2. Without changing the letter-name, raise each of the following notes one semitone.

3. Without changing the letter-name, lower each of the following notes one semitone.

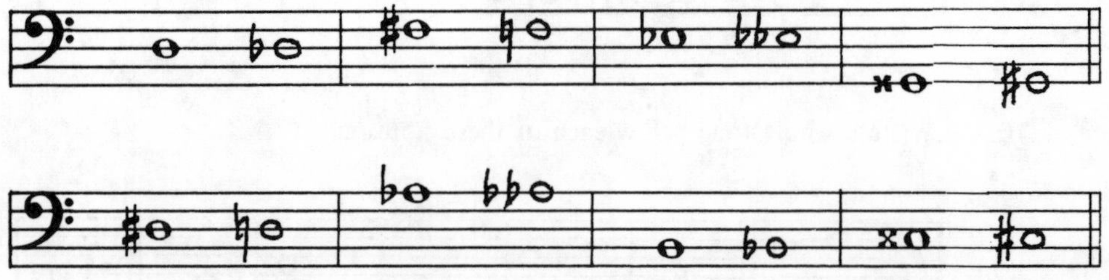

A B C EXERCISES (p. 16)

1. Write these scales in the treble clef ascending only, using accidentals instead of a key signature. Mark each semitone with a slur, and label the Tonic and Dominant notes.

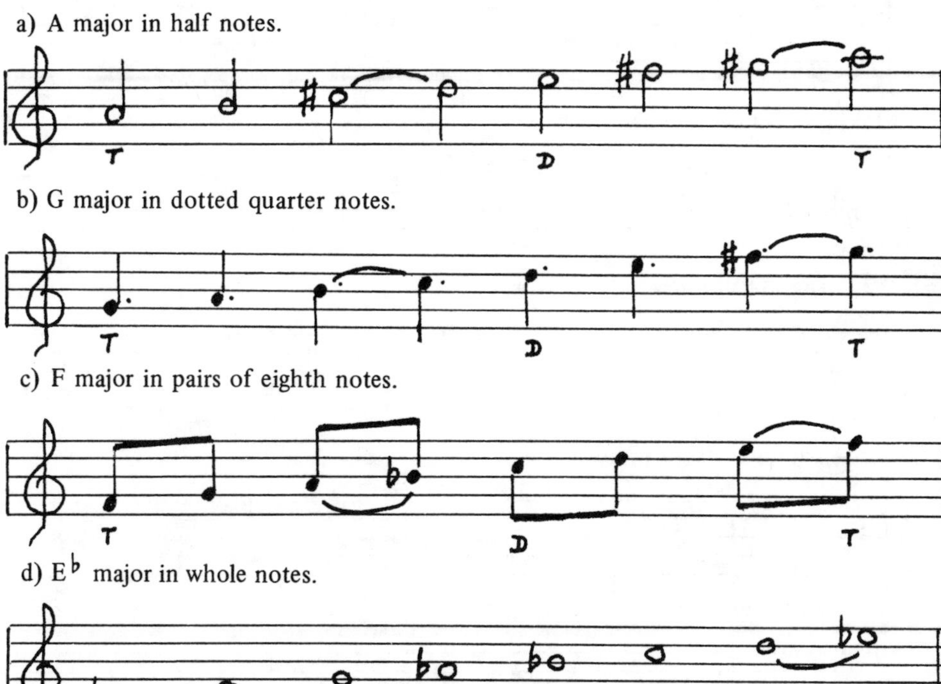

2. Write these scales in the bass clef ascending only, using the correct key signature for each. Mark each semitone with a slur, and label the Tonic and Dominant notes.

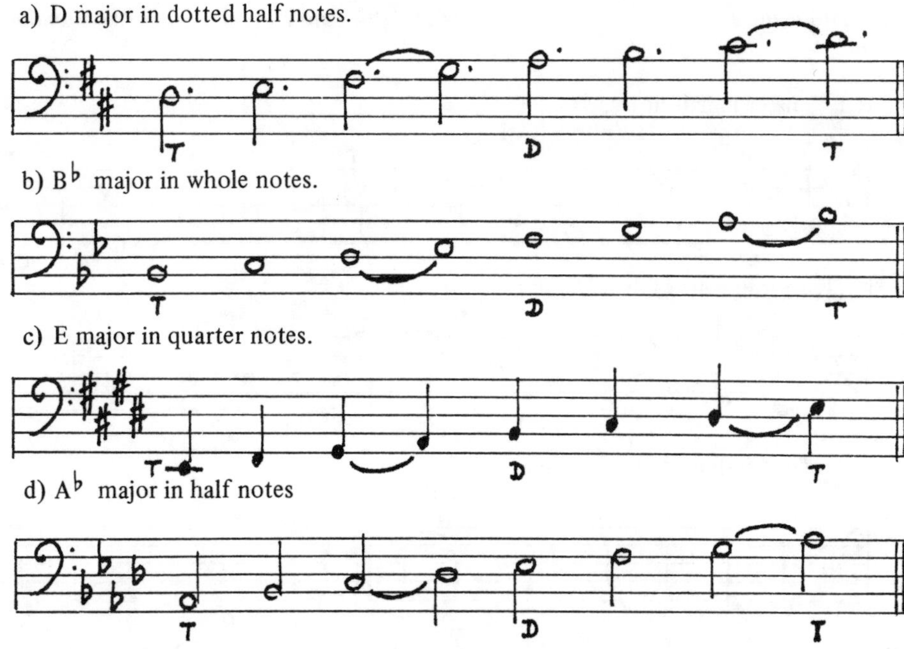

3. Write these scales in the treble clef ascending and descending using accidentals instead of a key-signature. Mark each semitone with a slur, and label the Tonic and Dominant notes.

4. Write these scales in the bass clef, ascending and descending, using the correct key signature for each. Mark each semitone with a slur, and label the Tonic and Dominant notes.

a) E♭ major in half notes.

c) F major in dotted quarter notes.

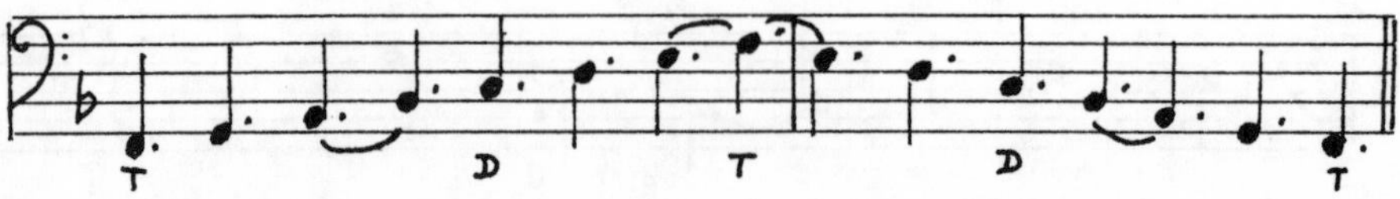

d) A major in whole notes.

5. Write these key signatures in the treble clef.

a) A$^{\flat}$ major c) B$^{\flat}$ major

b) E major d) D major

6. Write these key signatures in the bass clef.

a) F major c) E$^{\flat}$ major

b) A major d) G major

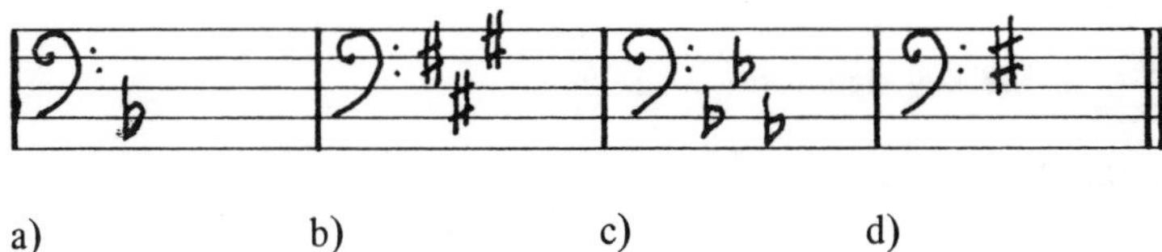

7. Write these notes in the treble clef, using the correct key signature for each.

a) the Tonic of F major f) the Dominant of G major

b) the Tonic of E$^{\flat}$ major g) the Tonic of A$^{\flat}$ major

c) the Dominant of D major h) the Dominant of E major

d) the Tonic of B$^{\flat}$ major i) the Dominant of C major

e) the Dominant of A major

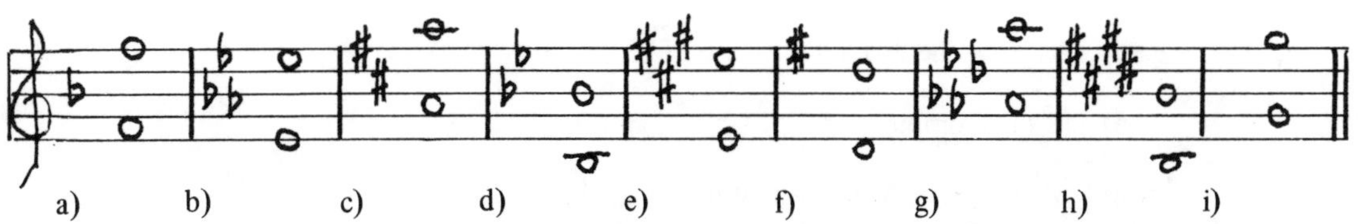

8. Write these notes in the bass clef, using the correct key signature for each.

a) the Tonic of C major
b) the Dominant of B♭ major
c) the Dominant of F major
d) the Tonic of D major
e) the Dominant of A♭ major
f) the Tonic of E major
g) the Tonic of G major
h) the Dominant of E♭ major
i) the Tonic of A major

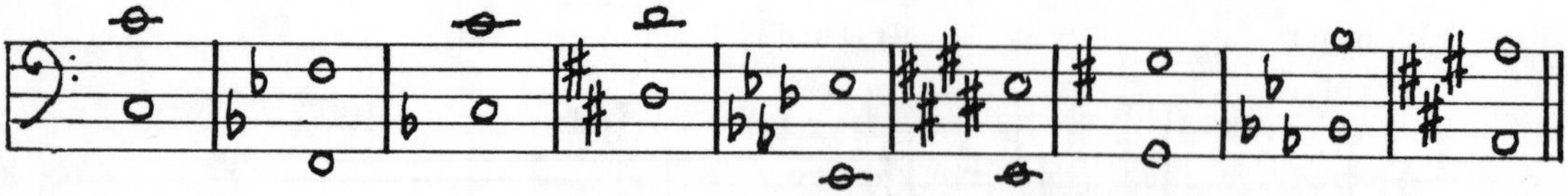

a) b) c) d) e) f) g) h) i)

9. Fill in the blanks in the following sentences.

a) the key signature of D major is 2 sharps F♯, C♯
b) the Tonic of E♭ major is E♭.
c) the key signature of A♭ major is 4 flats B♭, E♭, A♭, D♭
d) the key that has three sharps is A major
e)  [treble clef with one sharp] is the key signature of G major.
f) the key that has two flats is B♭ major
g) the order of the first four sharps is F♯ C♯ G♯ D♯
h) semitones occur between 3rd and 4th and 7th and 8th in every major scale.
i) the Dominant of C major is G
j) the names of the flats in E♭ major are B♭, E♭, A♭
k) the key signature of E major is 4 sharps F♯, C♯, G♯, D♯
l) D is the Dominant of G major.
m) the key that has four flats is A♭ major
n) the fifth note of any scale is called the Dominant
o) a scale can be divided into two Tetrachords
p) F is the Dominant of B♭ major.
q)  [bass clef with one flat] is the key signature of F major.
r) the order of tones and semitones in every major scale is T, T, ST, T, T, T, ST

s) E♭ is the Tonic of E♭ major.

t) the key that has no sharps or flats is C major.

B C MORE EXERCISES (p. 20)

1. Write the following notes in the treble clef, using the correct key signature for each.

a) the Mediant of B major
b) the Dominant of F♯ major
c) the Tonic of G♭ major
d) the Submediant of D major
e) the Supertonic of A major
f) the Leading-note of E♭ major
g) the Subdominant of C♯ major
h) the Dominant of A♭ major
i) the Supertonic of B♭ major
j) the Leading-note of E major

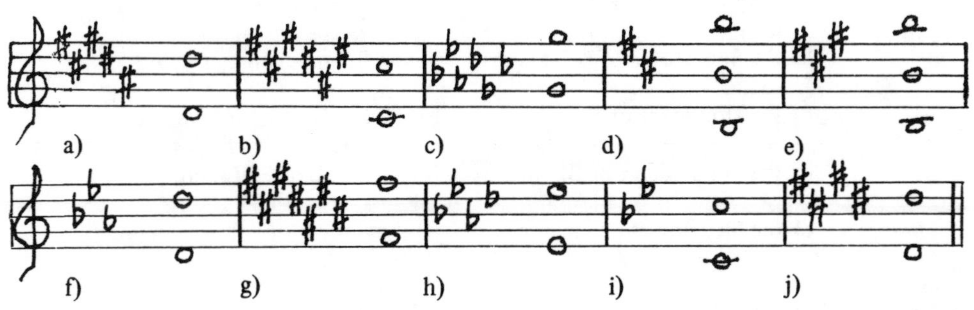

2. Write the following notes in the bass clef, using the correct key signature for each.

a) the Tonic of D♭ major
b) the Submediant of F major
c) the Supertonic of C major
d) the Dominant of E♭ major
e) the Leading-note of G major
f) the Mediant of F♯ major
g) the Subdominant of A major
h) the Submediant of A♭ major
i) the Mediant of B♭ major
j) the Tonic of B major

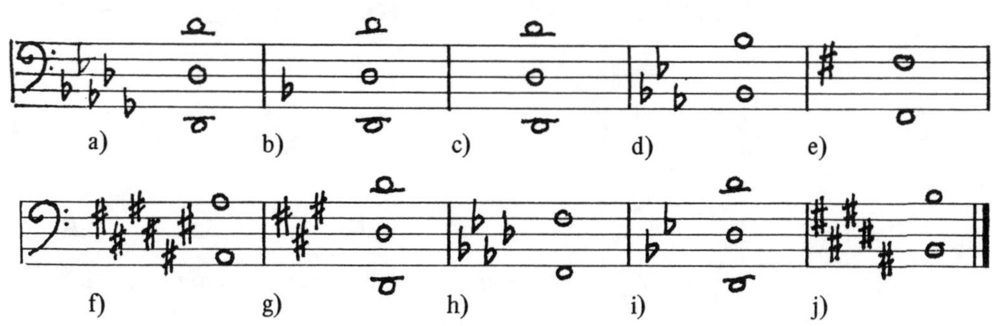

3. Write the following notes in the treble clef, using accidentals instead of a key signature.

a) the Subdominant of C major
b) the Tonic of E♭ major
c) the Dominant of D major
d) the Mediant of A major
e) the Submediant of G major
f) the Dominant of B major
g) the Supertonic of F major
h) the Subdominant of D♭ major
i) the Supertonic of A♭ major
j) the Leading-note of C♯ major

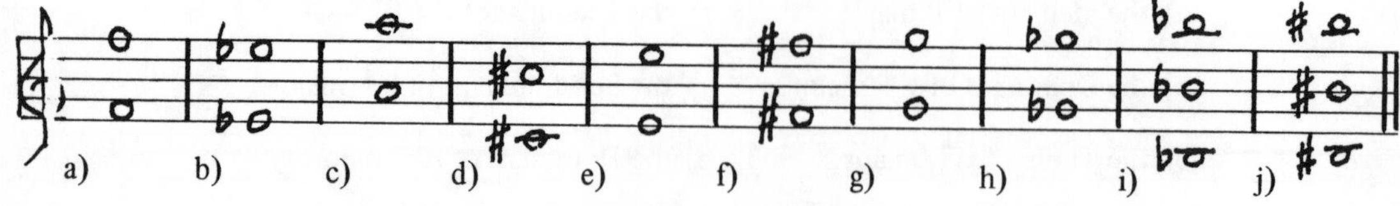

4. Write these notes in the bass clef, using accidentals instead of a key signature.

a) the Leading-note of A major
b) the Supertonic of G♭ major
c) the Dominant of E major
d) the Submediant of B♭ major
e) the Mediant of C♯ major
f) the Leading-note of B major
g) the Submediant of C major
h) the Supertonic of D major
i) the Tonic of F♯ major
j) the Subdominant of G major

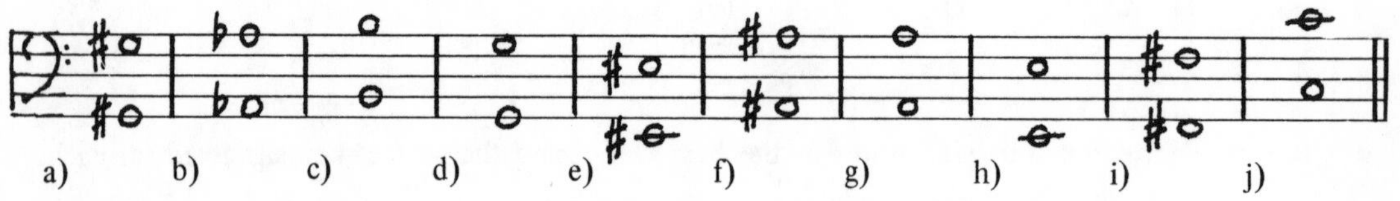

5. Name the major key, and the technical name of the degree of each of the following.

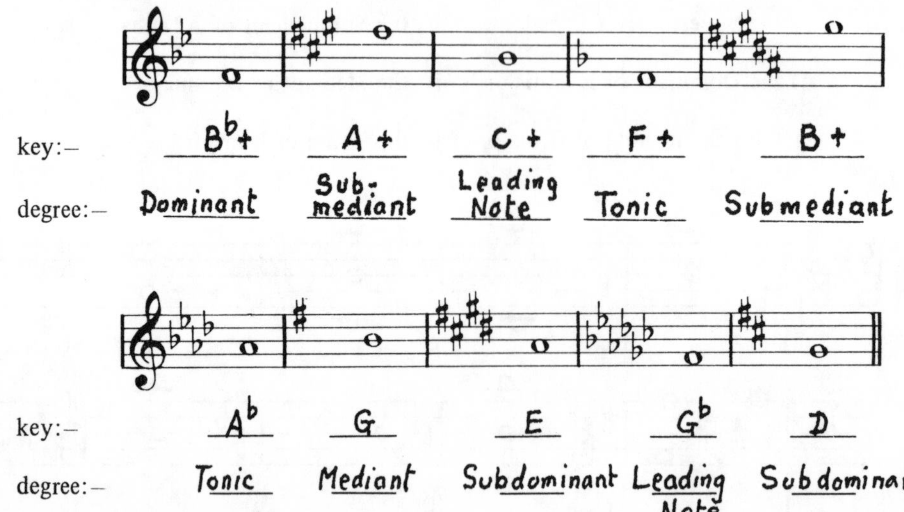

6. Name the major key and the technical name of the degree of each of the following.

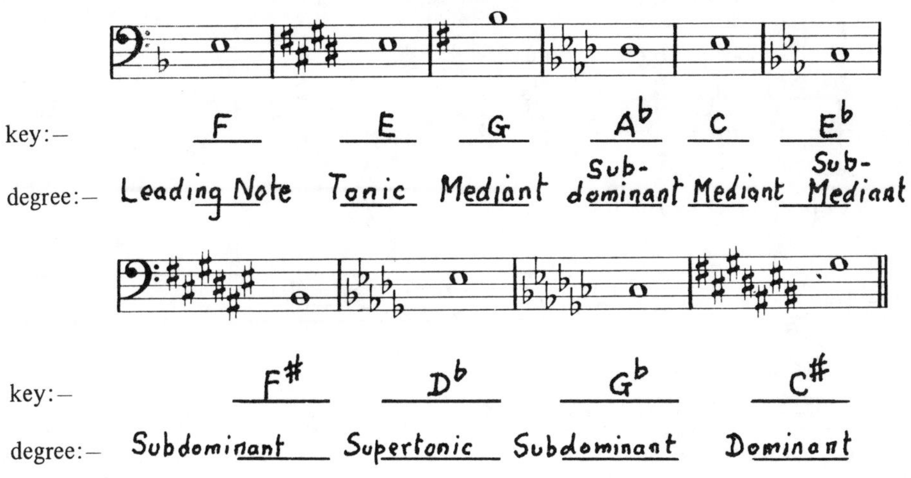

7. List the order of the sharps as they appear in a key signature.

F♯ C♯ G♯ D♯ A♯ E♯ B♯

8. List the order of the flats as they appear in a key signature.

B♭ E♭ A♭ D♭ G♭ C♭ F♭

9. Write these scales ascending and descending in the treble clef. Use accidentals instead of a key signature and mark the semitones with a slur.

a) F♯ major in half notes.

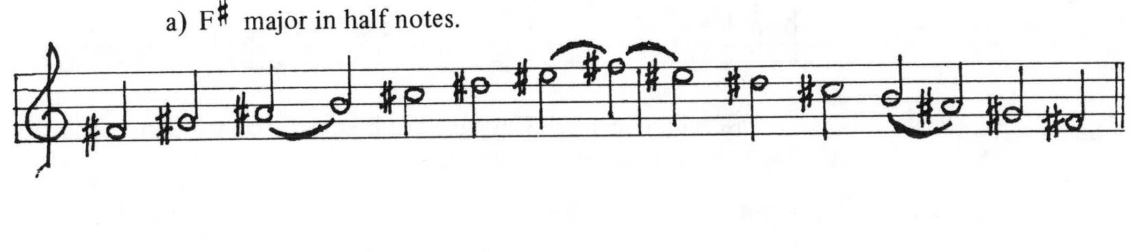

b) C♭ major in quarter notes.

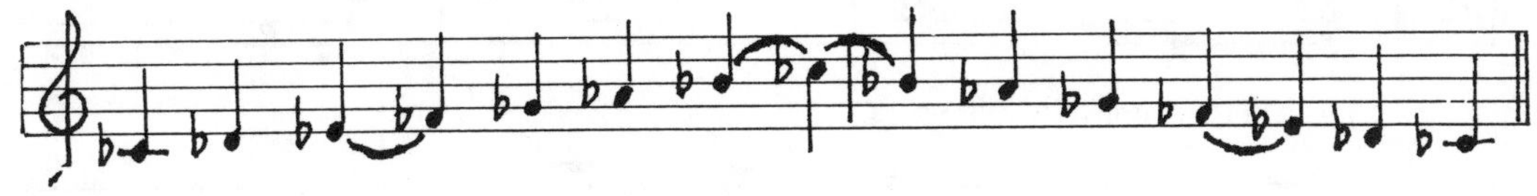

c) D♭ major in eighth notes.

10. Write these scales ascending and descending in the treble clef. Use the correct key signature for each, and mark the semitones with a slur.
a) C♯ major in sixteenth notes.
b) B major in half notes.
c) G♭ major in whole notes.
11. Write these scales ascending and descending in the bass clef. Use accidentals instead of a key signature, and mark the semitones with a slur.
a) B major in quarter notes.
b) C♯ major in eighth notes.
c) G♭ major in dotted half notes.
12. Write these scales ascending and descending in the bass clef. Use the correct key signature for each, and mark the semitones with a slur.
a) F♯ major in dotted quarter notes.
b) D♭ major in whole notes.
c) C♭ major in sixteenth notes.

13. Write these scales in the treble clef, ascending only, using the correct key signature for each.

    a) the major scale whose key signature is 5 flats.

    b) the major scale whose dominant is G♯ .

    c) the major scale whose leading-note is A♯ .

    d) the major scale whose key-signature is 6 flats.

    e) the major scale whose supertonic is G♯ .

    f) the major scale whose mediant is E♭ .

    g) the major scale whose subdominant is F♯ .

    h) the major scale whose submediant is G♯ .

    i) the major scale whose leading-note is F.

    j) the major scale whose mediant is G.

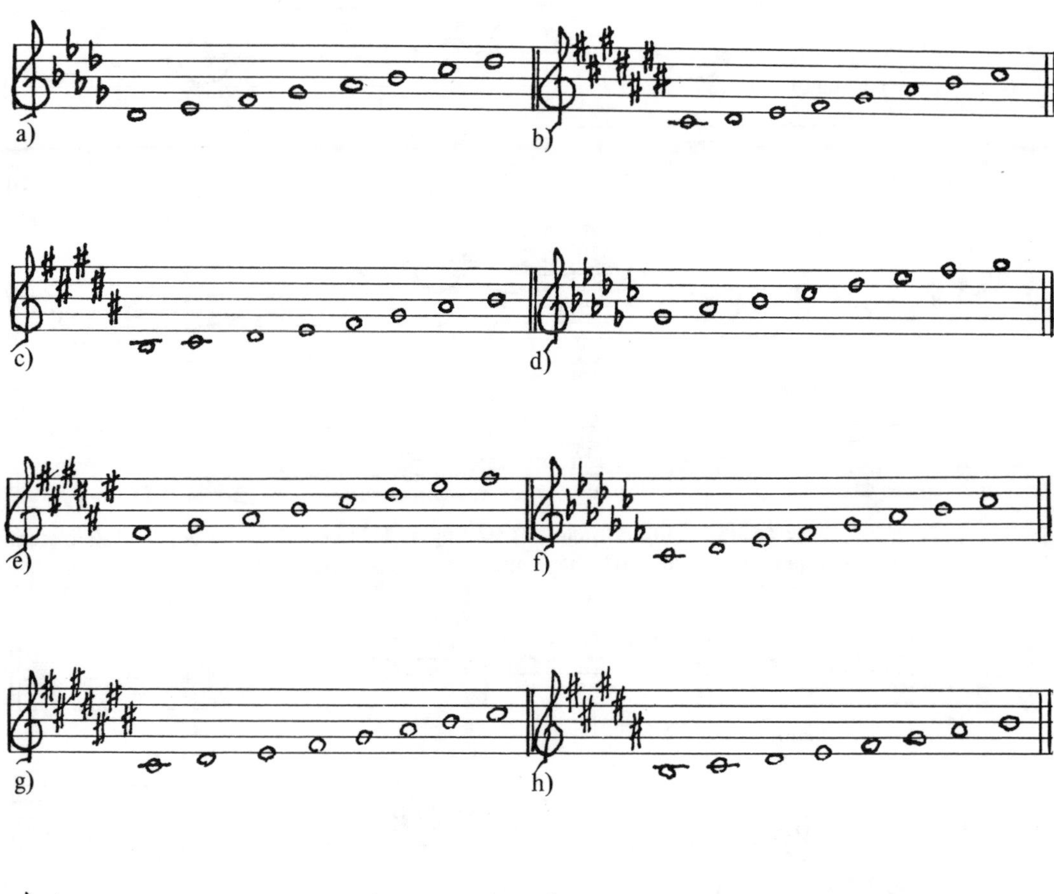

C STILL MORE EXERCISES (p. 24)

1. Write these scales in the alto clef, ascending and descending, using the correct key signature for each, and marking the semitones with a slur.

a) B♭ major

b) D major

c) G♭ major

d) C♯ major

e) F major

f) B major

g) E♭ major

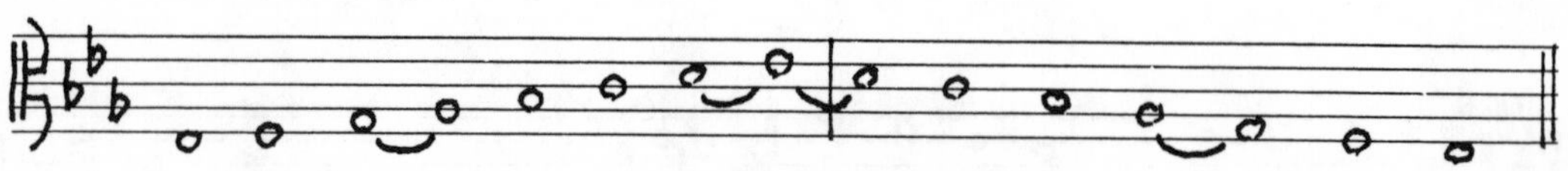

2. Write these scales in the alto clef, ascending and descending. Use accidentals instead of a key signature, and mark the semitones with a slur.

a) A major

b) D♭ major

c) F♯ major

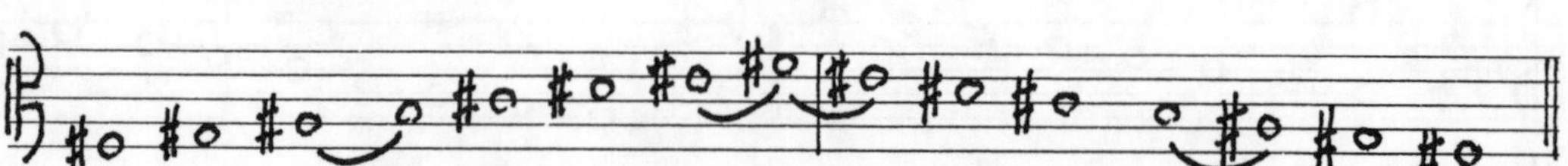

d) C major

e) A♭ major

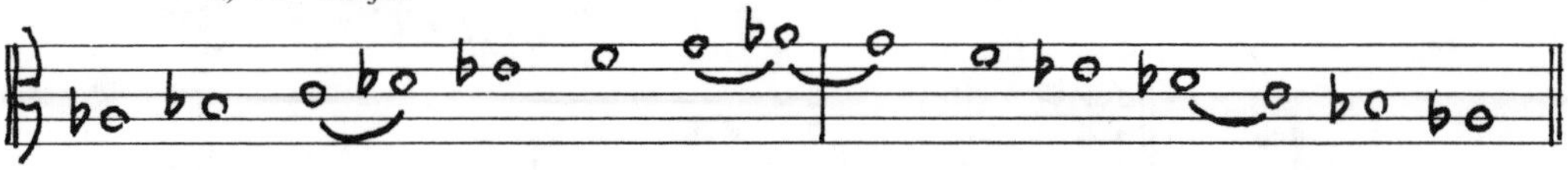

f) E major

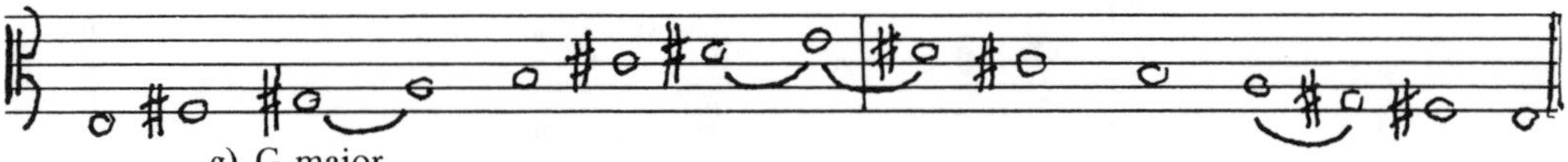

g) G major

3. Write these scales in the tenor clef, descending only. Use the correct key signature for each, and mark the semitones with a slur.

a) C major

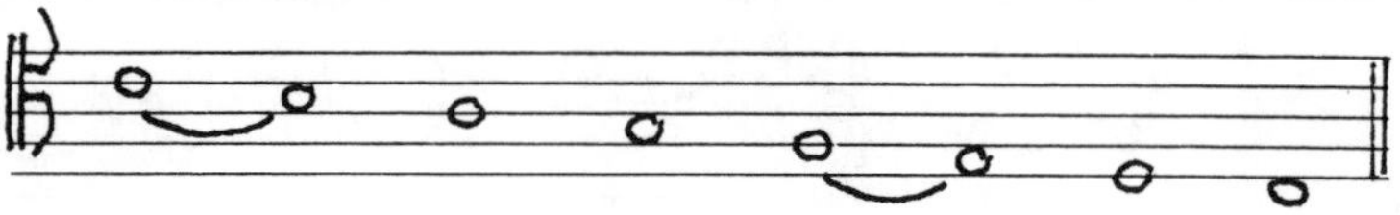

b) E major

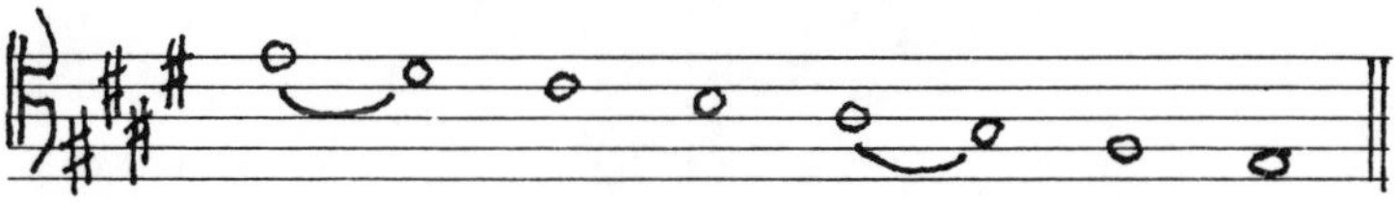

c) G major

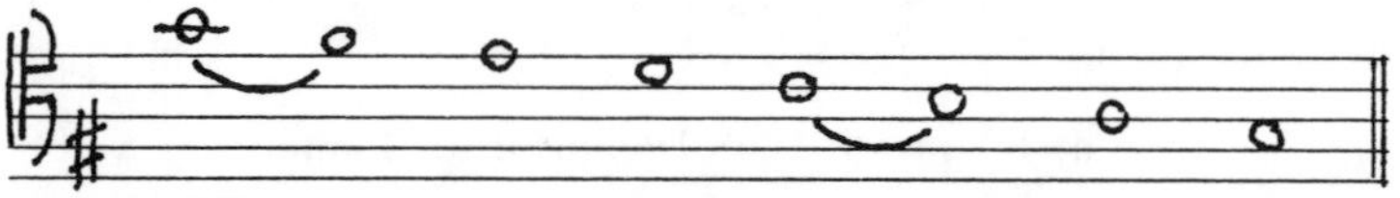

d) A major

e) D♭ major

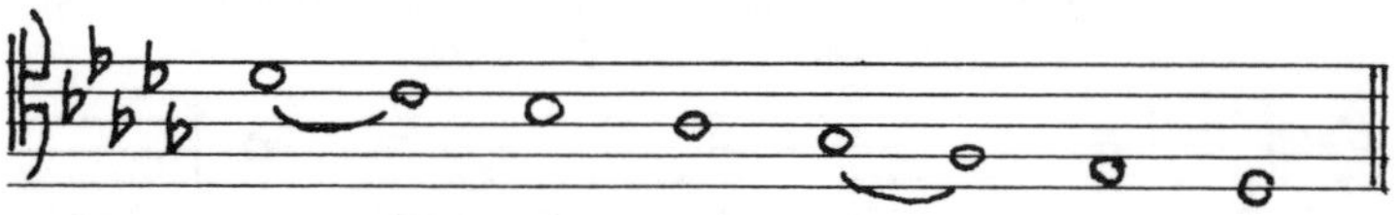

f) F♯ major

g) A♭ major

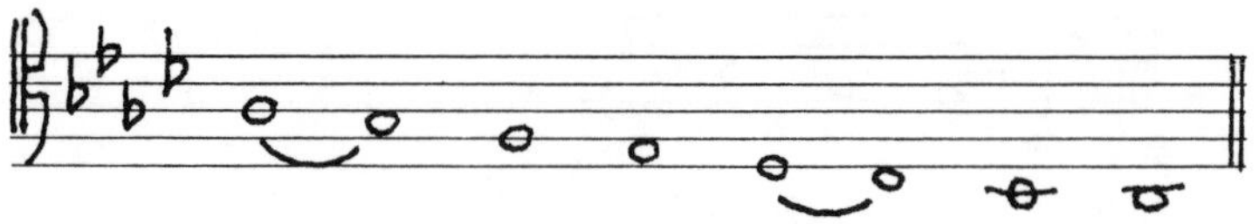

4. Write these scales in the tenor clef, descending only. Use accidentals instead of a key signature, and mark the semitones with a slur.

a) C♯ major

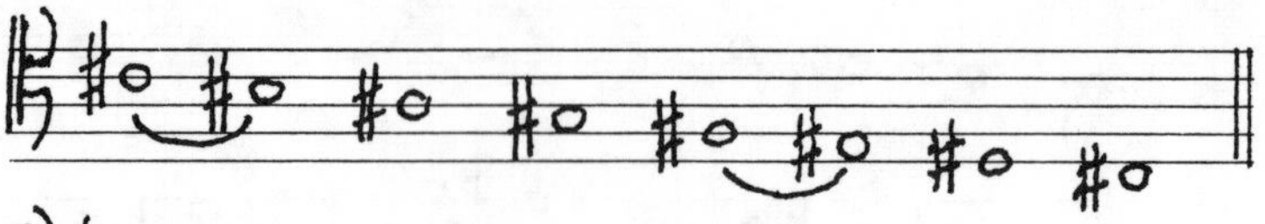

b) E♭ major

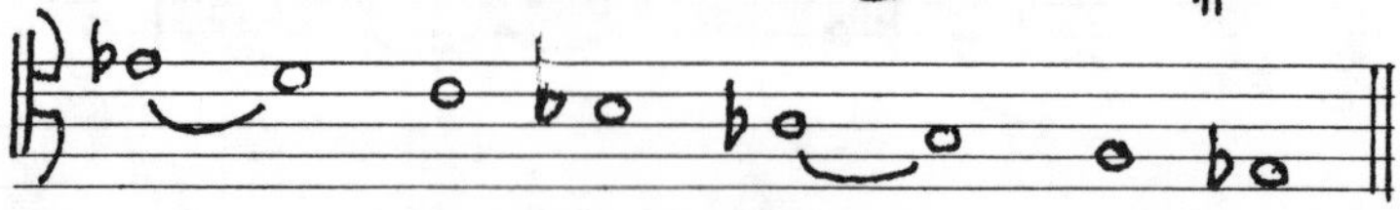

c) F major

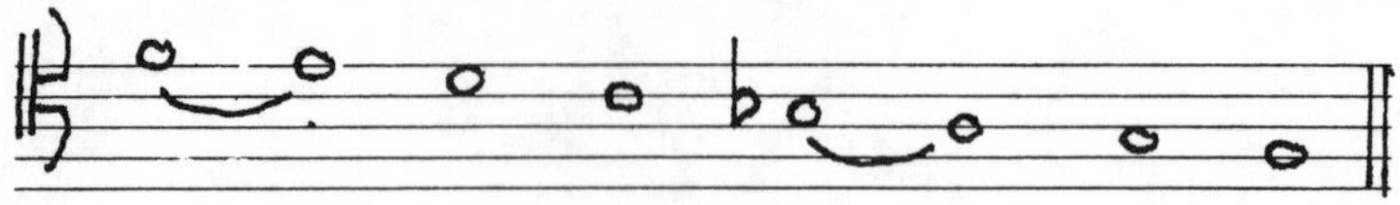

d) B major

e) B♭ major

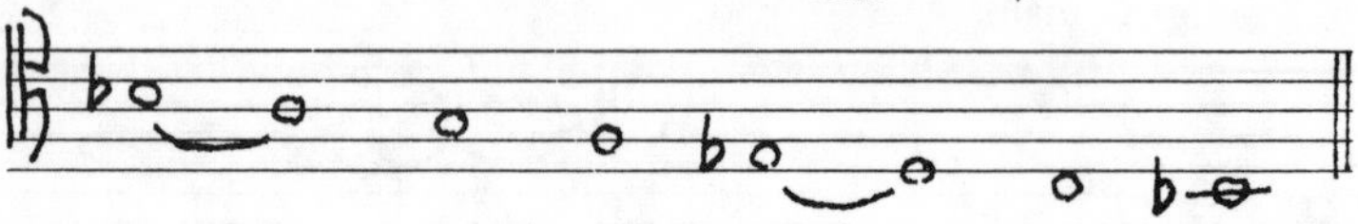

f) D major

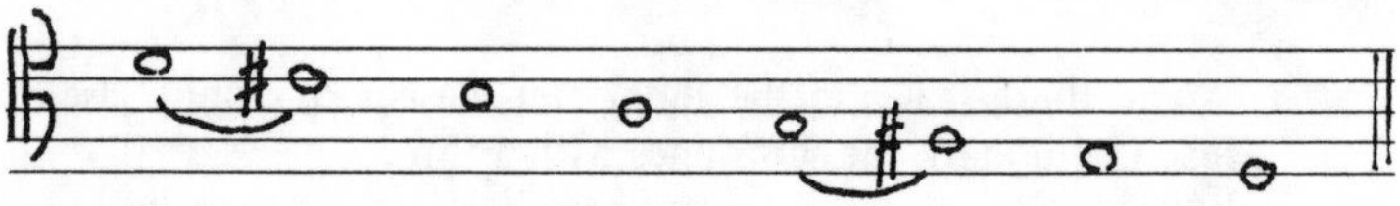

g) G♭ major

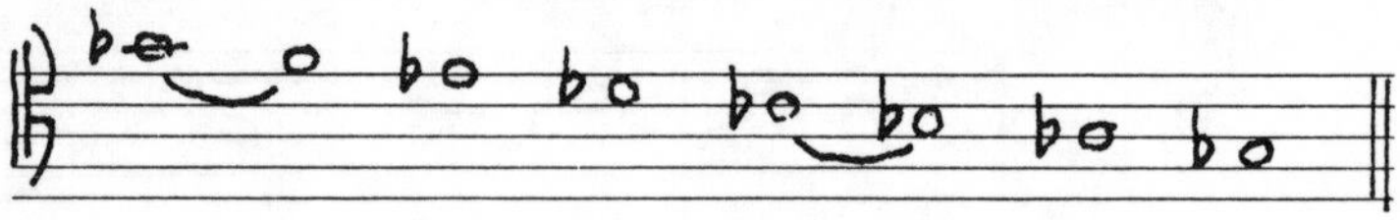

5. Write the following scales for one octave in the bass clef, ascending and descending. Use the correct key signature, and mark the semitones with a slur.

a) B♭ major, from Dominant to Dominant.

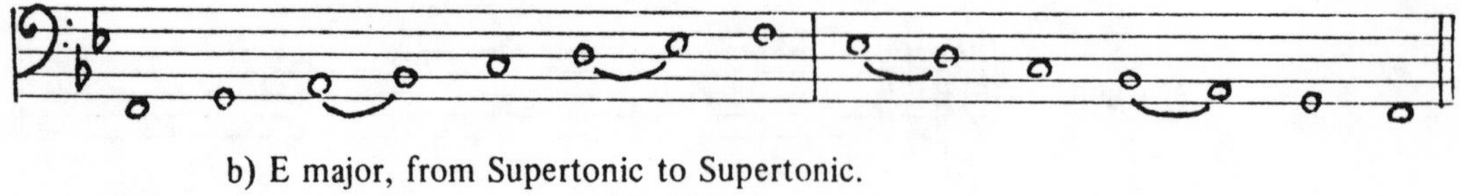

b) E major, from Supertonic to Supertonic.

c) D♭ major, from Subdominant to Subdominant.

d) G major, from Submediant to Submediant.

e) C# major, from Tonic to Tonic.

6. Write the following scales for one octave in the treble clef, ascending and descending. Use accidentals instead of a key signature, and mark the semitones with a slur.

a) A major, from Mediant to Mediant.

Unless specified, any kind of note is acceptable.

b) F# major, from Tonic to Tonic.

c) E♭ major from Dominant to Dominant.

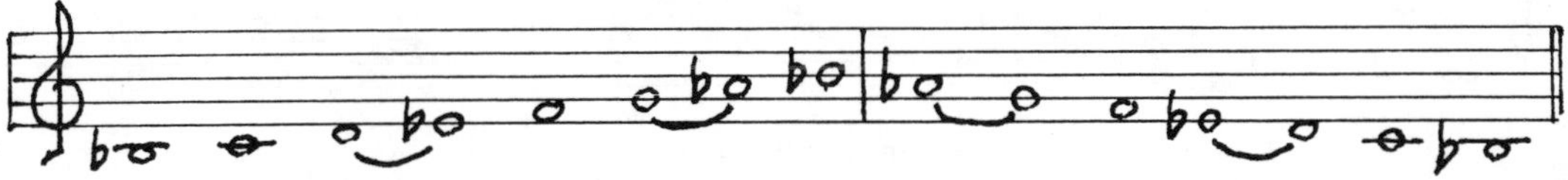

d) D major, from Leading-note to Leading-note.

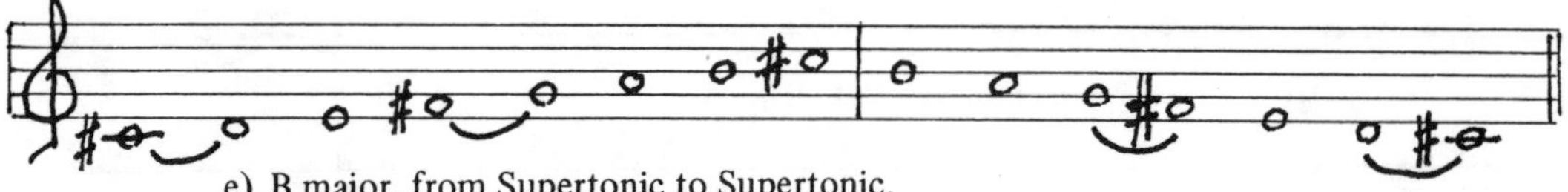

e) B major, from Supertonic to Supertonic.

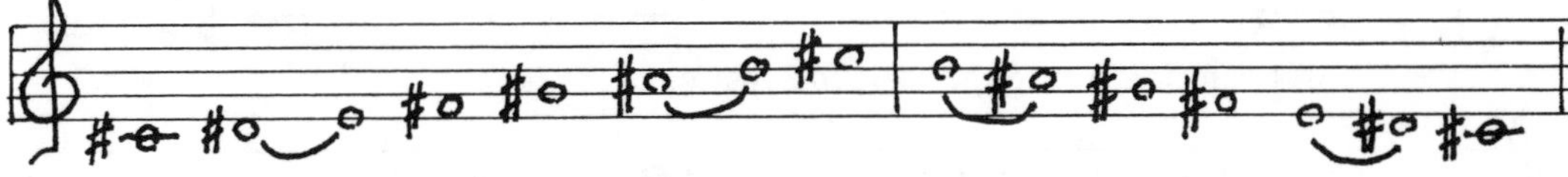

7. Write these scales in the alto clef for one octave, ascending and descending. Use the correct key signature, and mark the semitones with a slur.

a) A♭ major, from Dominant to Dominant.

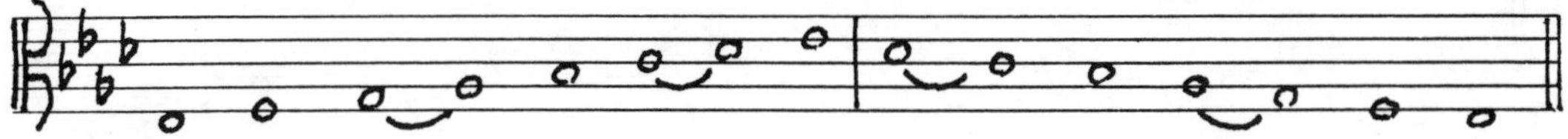

b) F♯ major, from Leading-note to Leading-note.

c) G♭ major, from Supertonic to Supertonic.

d) B major, from Subdominant to Subdominant.

e) A major, from Submediant to Submediant.

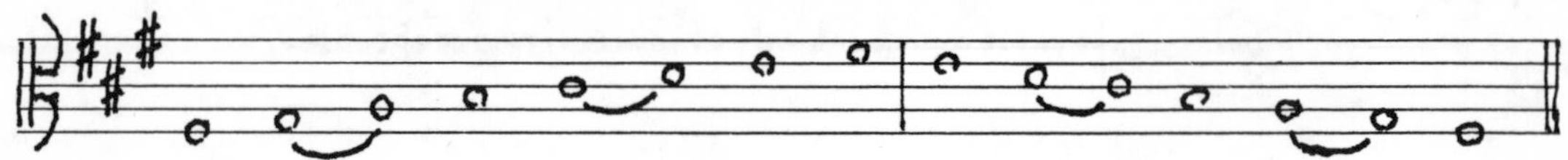

8. Write these scales for one octave in the tenor clef, ascending and descending. Use accidentals instead of a key signature, and mark the semitones with a slur.

a) D♭ major, from Tonic to Tonic.

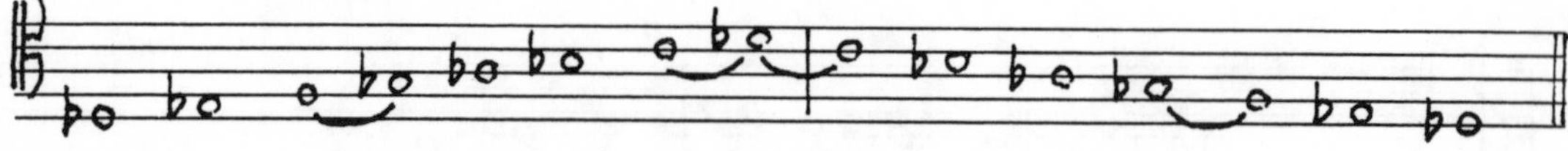

b) E major, from Submediant to Submediant.

c) F major, from Mediant to Mediant.

d) C♯ major, from Supertonic to Supertonic.

e) B♭ major, from Leading-note to Leading-note.

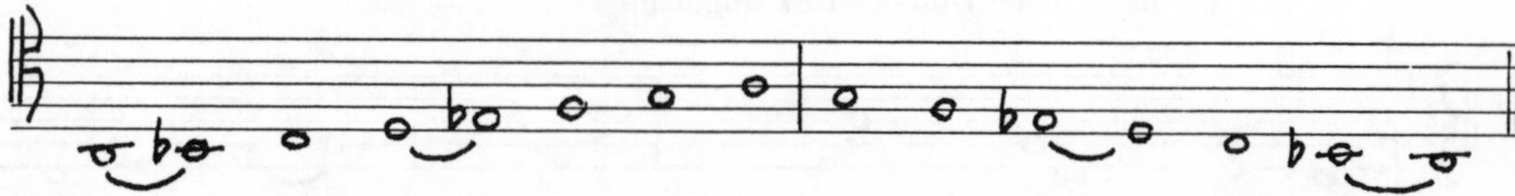

A B C EXERCISES (p. 34)

1. Name the relative major of the following minor keys.

a) C# minor E + d) B minor D+

b) A minor C + e) G minor B♭ +

c) F minor A♭ + f) E minor G +

2. Name the relative minor of the following major keys.

a) A major F# – d) E major C# –

b) E♭ major C – e) G major E –

c) F major D – f) B♭ major G –

3. Fill in the blanks in the following sentences.

a) the minor key whose key signature is one sharp is E –

b) the key signature of B minor is 2 sharps F#, C#.

c) the key signature of A major is 3 sharps F#, C#, G#.

d) the major key whose key signature is four flats is A♭ +

e) the Dominant of D minor is A

f) the minor key whose key signature is three sharps is F# –

g) the key signature of E♭ major is 3 Flats B♭, E♭, A♭

h) the Dominant of F# minor is C#

i) the major key whose key signature is two flats is B♭ +

j) the key signature of F minor is 4 Flats B♭, E♭, A♭, D♭

k) the minor key whose key signature is two flats is G –

l) the major key whose key signature is one sharp is G +

m) the key signature of C# minor is 4 sharps F#, C#, G#, D#

n) the Dominant of B minor is F#

o) the key signature of F major is 1 Flat B♭

p) the key signature of D minor is 1 Flat B♭

q) the major key whose key signature is four sharps is E +

r) the minor key whose key signature is three flats is C –

s) the key signature of D major is 2 sharps F#, C#

t) the Dominant of C# minor is G#

4. Write these scales in the treble clef, ascending and descending. Use the correct key signature for each, and label the Tonic and Dominant notes.

a) A minor harmonic

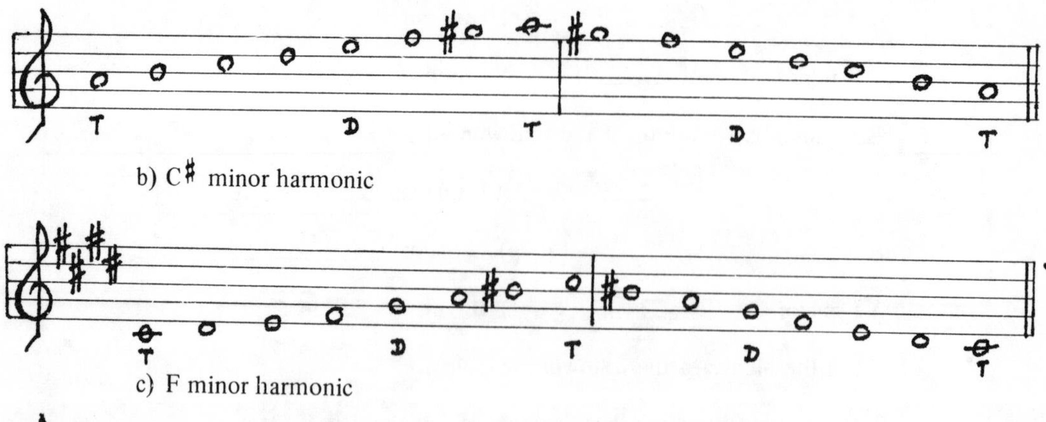

b) C♯ minor harmonic

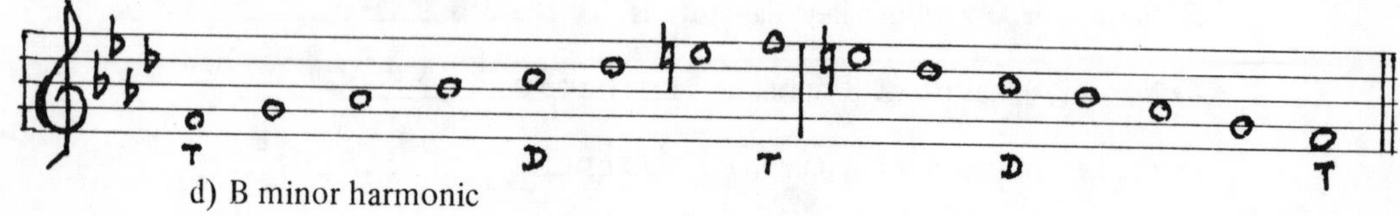

c) F minor harmonic

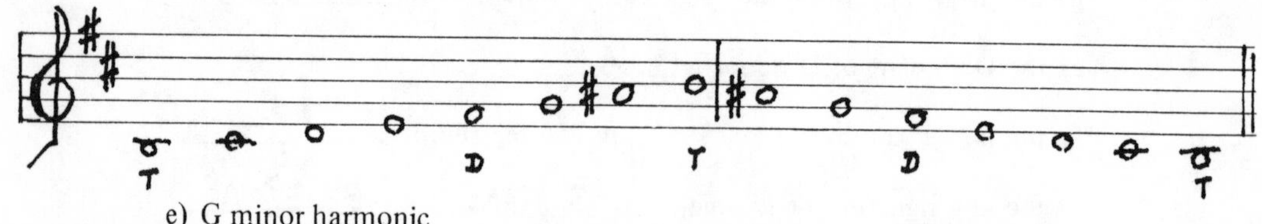

d) B minor harmonic

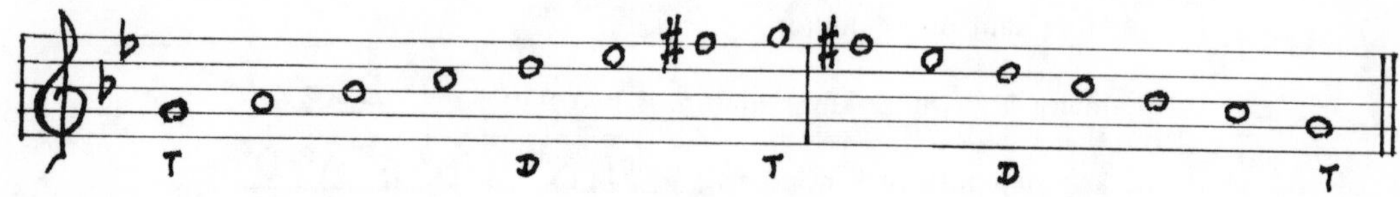

e) G minor harmonic

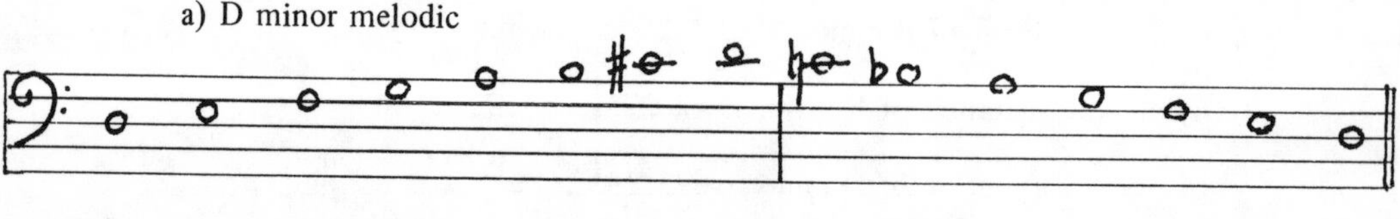

5. Write these scales in the bass clef, ascending and descending. Use accidentals instead of a key signature.

a) D minor melodic

b) E minor melodic

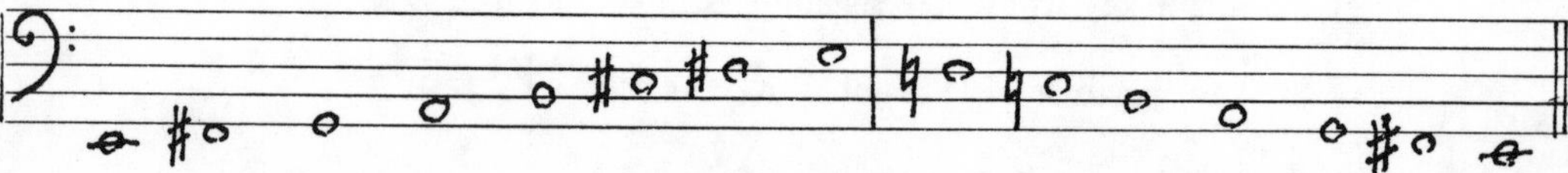

c) C minor melodic

d) F♯ minor melodic

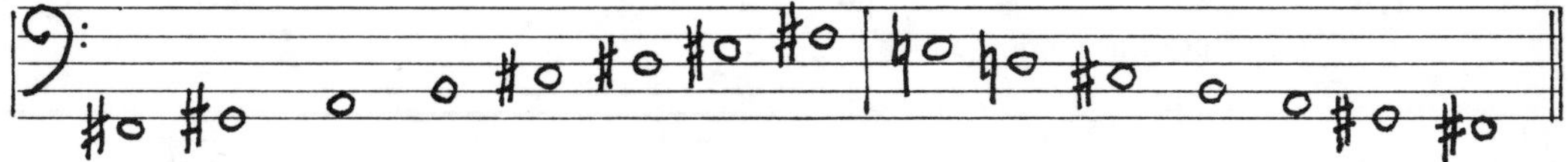

6. Write these scales in the treble clef, ascending and descending. Use accidentals instead of a key signature.

a) B minor melodic

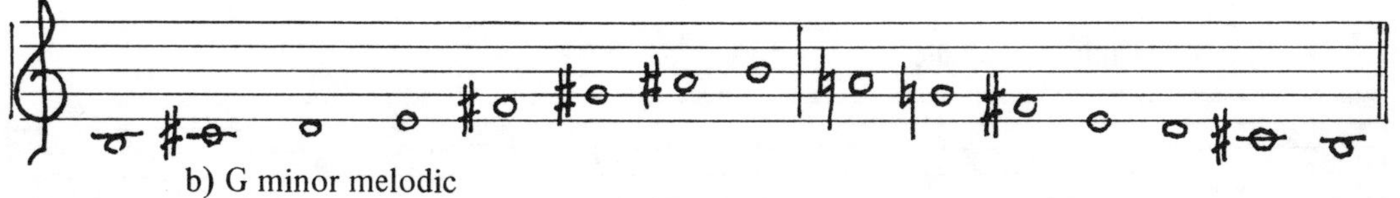

b) G minor melodic

c) A minor melodic

d) C♯ minor melodic

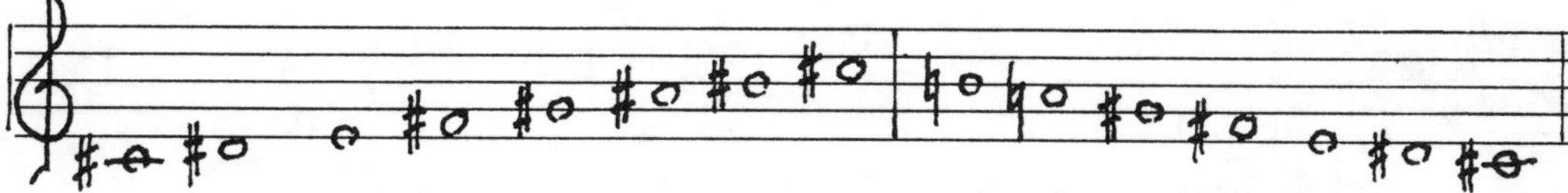

e) F minor melodic

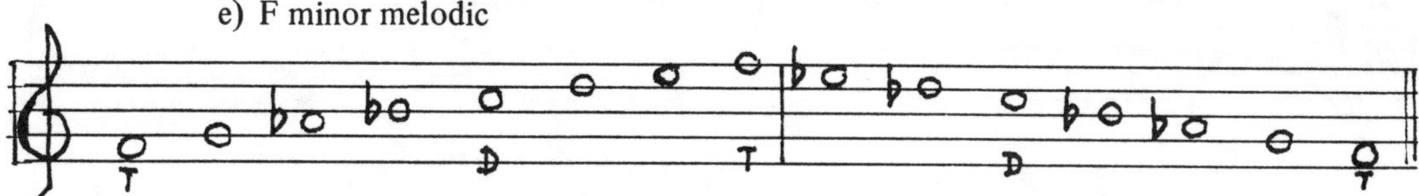

7. Write these scales in the bass clef, ascending and descending. Use the correct key-signature and label the Dominant and Tonic notes.

a) C minor harmonic

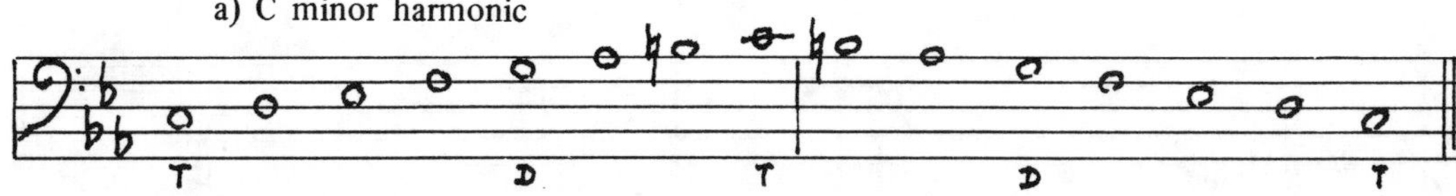

b) F# minor harmonic

c) E minor harmonic

d) D minor harmonic

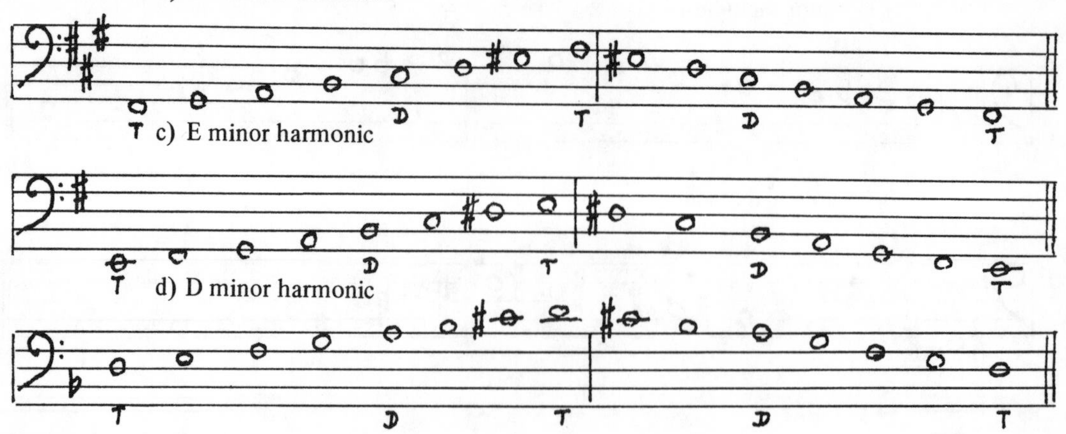

8. Write these scales in the bass clef, ascending and descending. Use the correct key-signature for each and mark the semitones with a slur.

a) G minor melodic

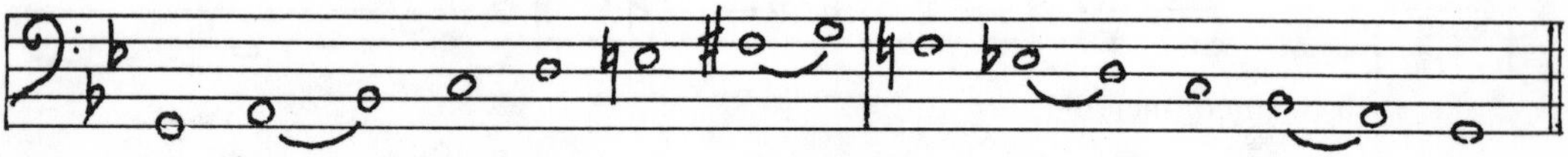

b) A minor melodic

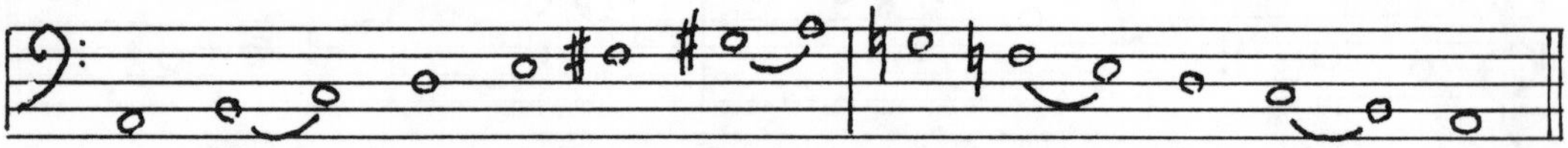

c) B minor melodic

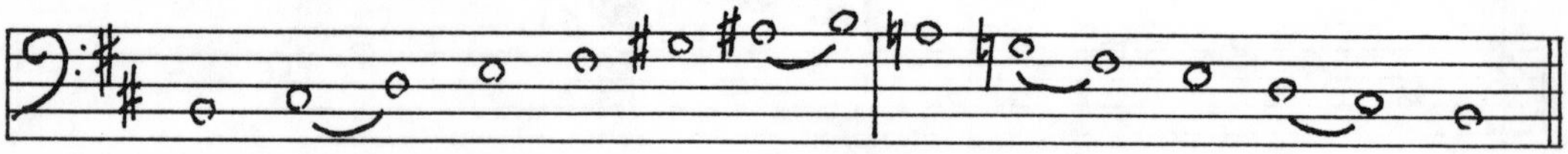

d) F minor melodic

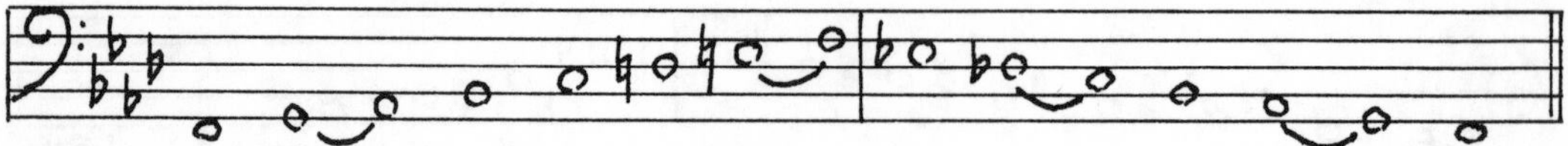

e) C# minor melodic

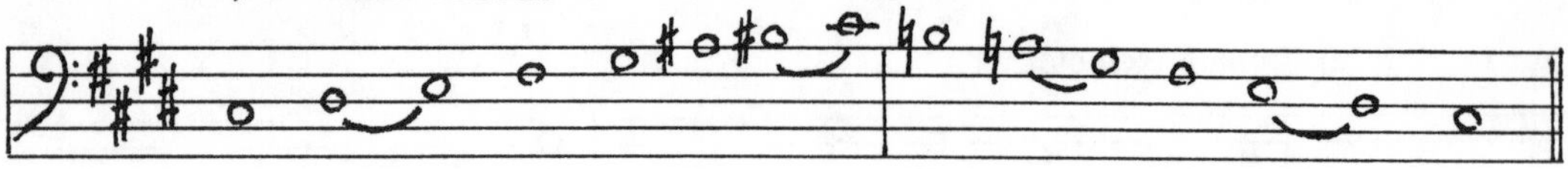

9. Write these scales in the treble clef, ascending and descending. Use accidentals instead of a key signature, and mark the semitones with a slur.

a) E minor harmonic

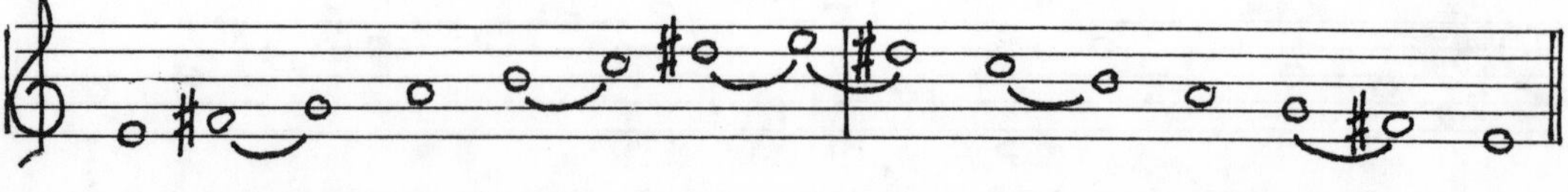

b) D minor harmonic

c) F# minor harmonic

d) C minor harmonic

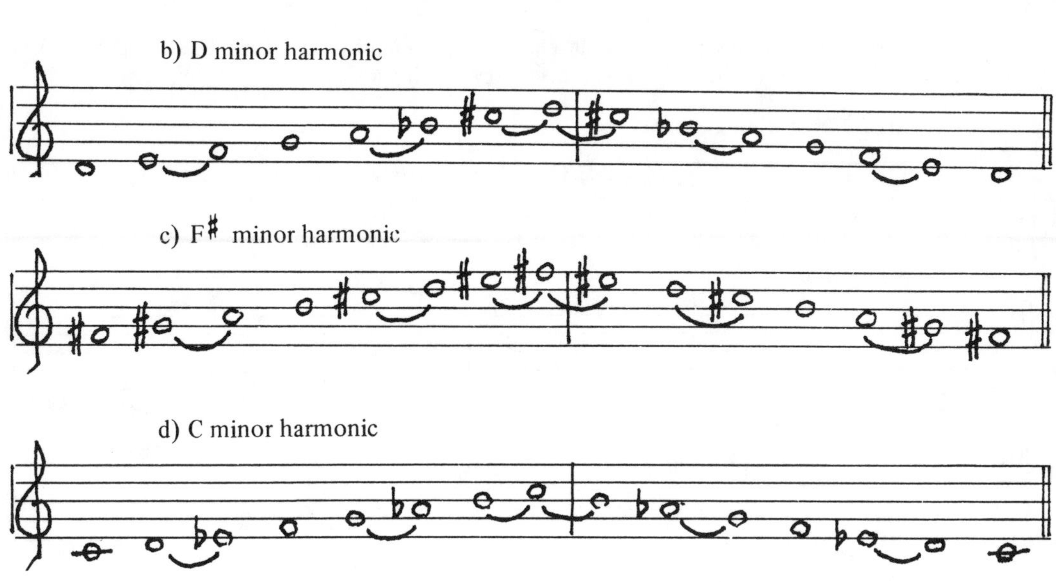

10. Write these scales in the bass clef, ascending and descending. Use accidentals instead of a key signature, and mark the semitones with a slur.

a) C# minor harmonic

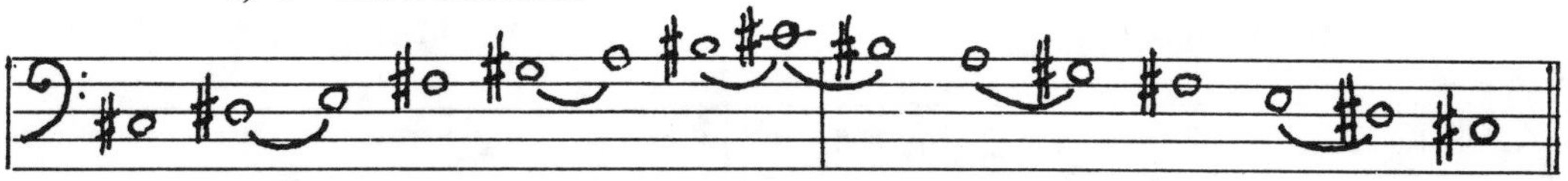

b) F minor harmonic

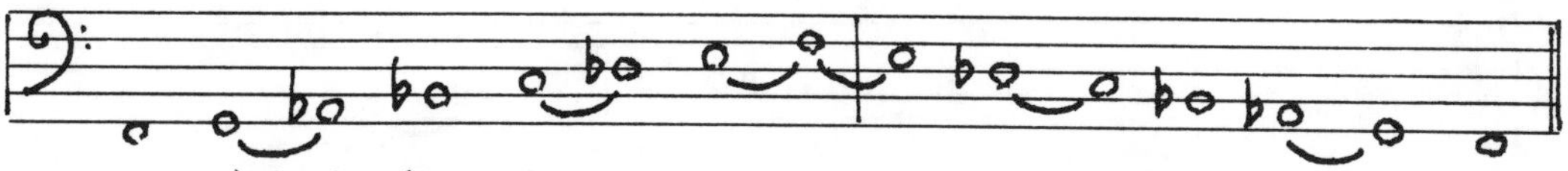

c) A minor harmonic

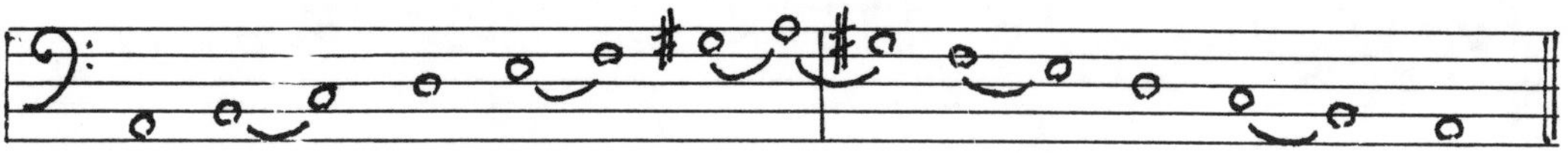

d) G minor harmonic

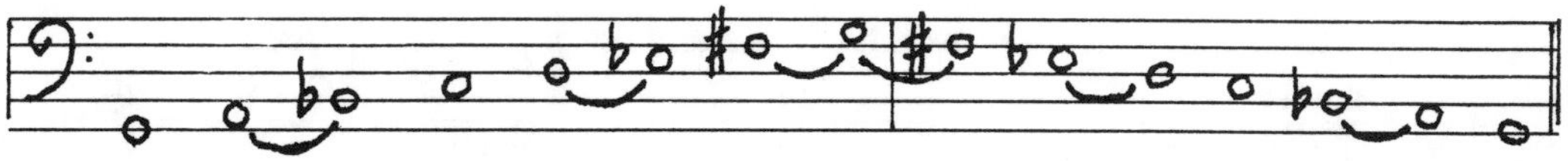

e) B minor harmonic

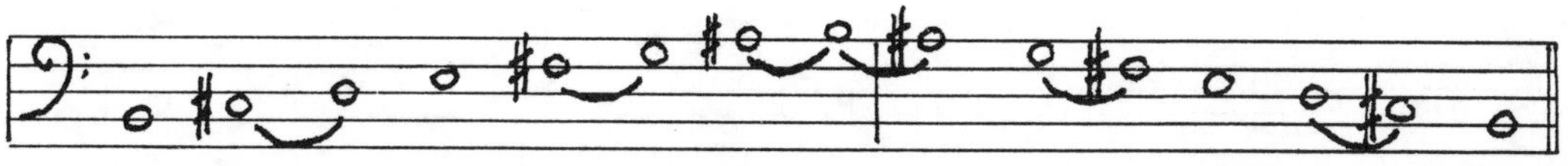

11. Write these scales in the treble clef, ascending and descending. Use the correct key-signature for each, and mark the semitones with a slur.

a) F♯ minor melodic

b) C minor melodic

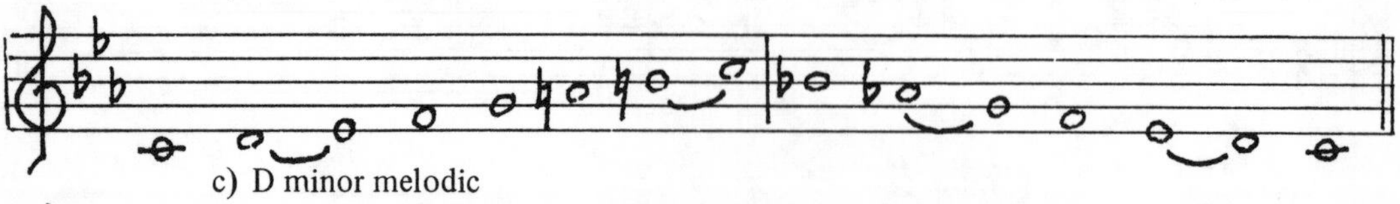

c) D minor melodic

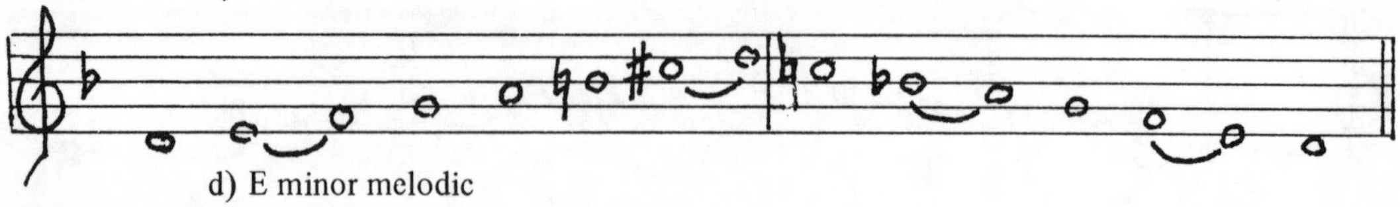

d) E minor melodic

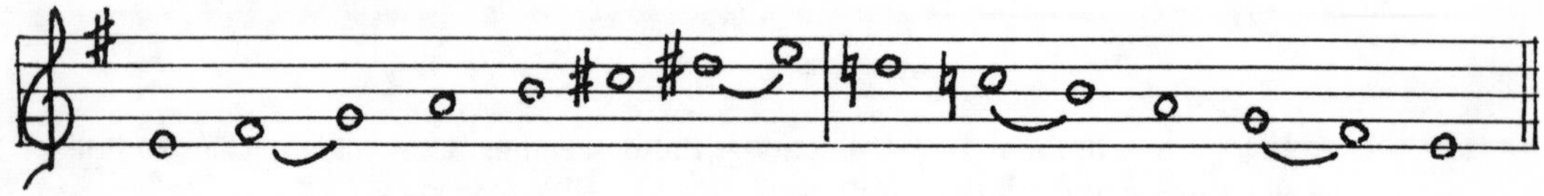

B C MORE EXERCISES (p. 39)

1. Write these scales in the treble clef, ascending and descending. Use the correct key-signature for each and mark the semitones with a slur.

a) D♯ minor melodic

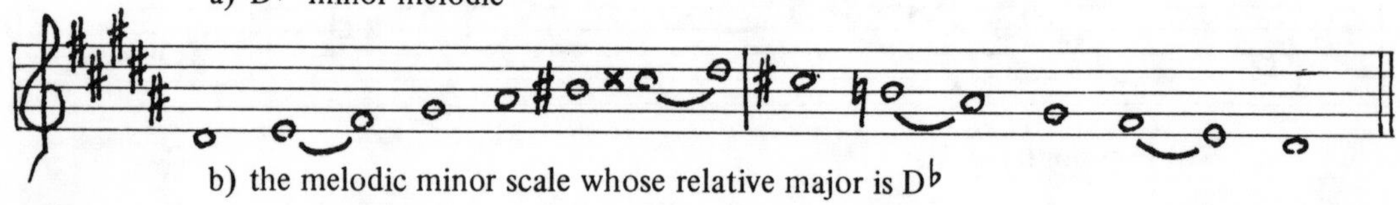

b) the melodic minor scale whose relative major is D♭

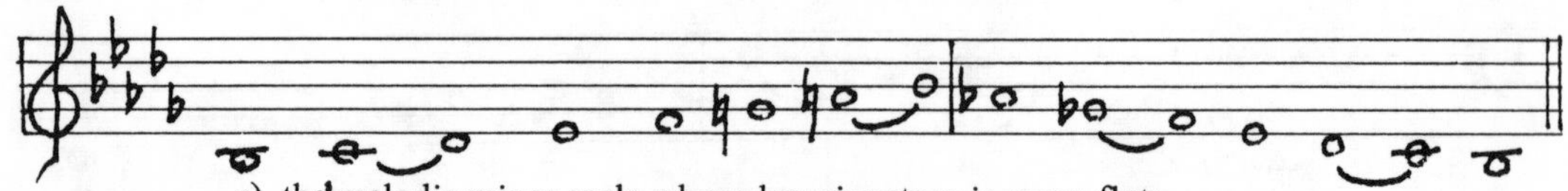

c) the melodic minor scale whose key signature is seven flats.

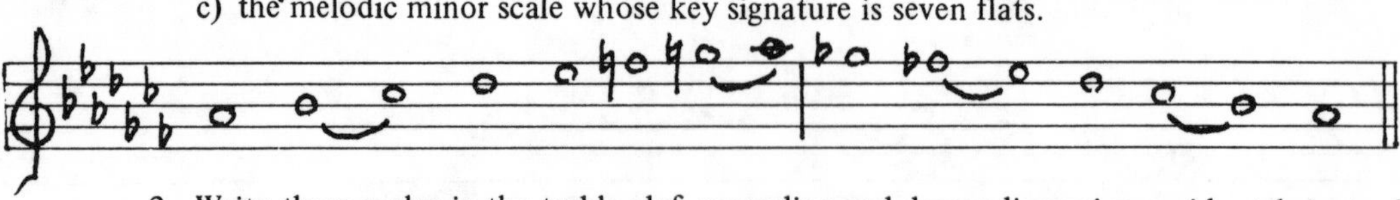

2. Write these scales in the treble clef, ascending and descending using accidentals instead of a key signature. Mark the semitones with a slur.

a) A♯ minor melodic

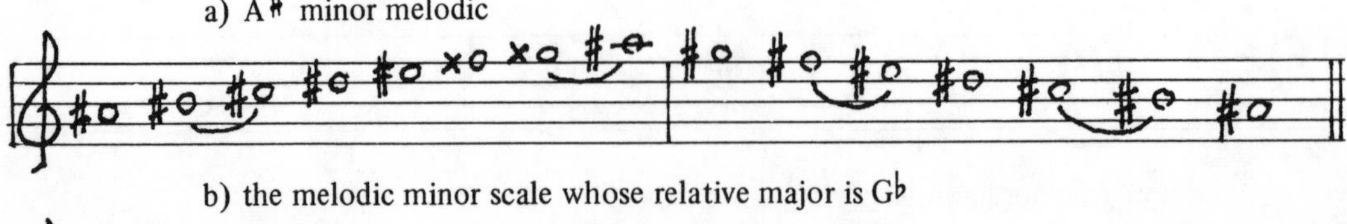

b) the melodic minor scale whose relative major is G♭

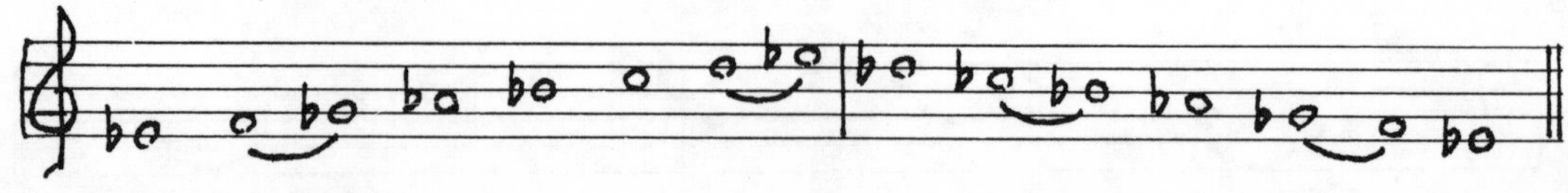

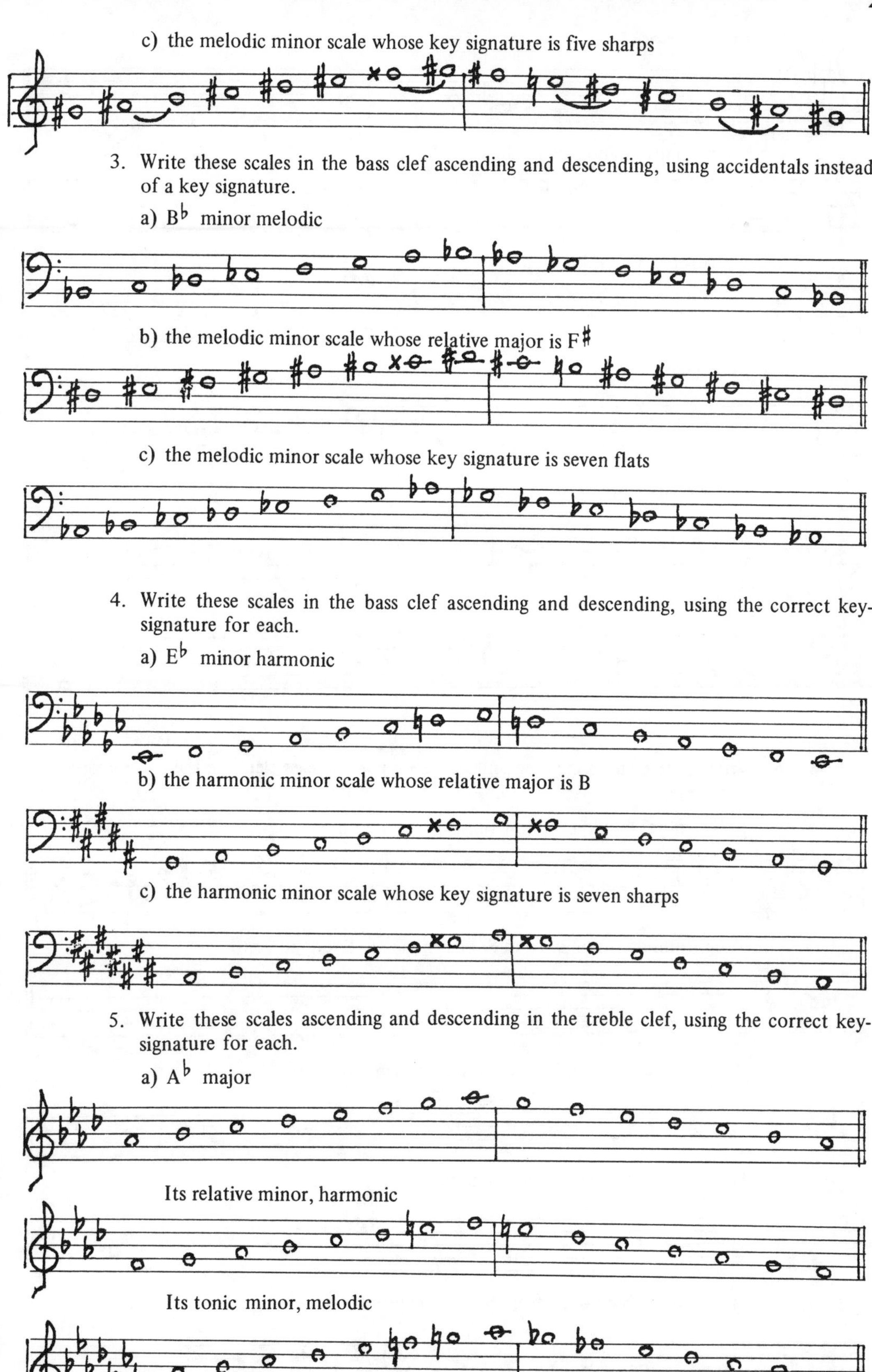
c) the melodic minor scale whose key signature is five sharps
3. Write these scales in the bass clef ascending and descending, using accidentals instead of a key signature.
a) B♭ minor melodic
b) the melodic minor scale whose relative major is F♯
c) the melodic minor scale whose key signature is seven flats
4. Write these scales in the bass clef ascending and descending, using the correct key-signature for each.
a) E♭ minor harmonic
b) the harmonic minor scale whose relative major is B
c) the harmonic minor scale whose key signature is seven sharps
5. Write these scales ascending and descending in the treble clef, using the correct key-signature for each.
a) A♭ major
Its relative minor, harmonic
Its tonic minor, melodic

b) B♭ major
Its relative minor, melodic
Its tonic minor, harmonic
c) F major
Its relative minor, harmonic
Its tonic minor, melodic
6. Write these scales ascending and descending in the bass clef. Use the correct key-signature for each, and mark the semitones with a slur.
a) G♯ minor melodic, from Dominant to Dominant
b) C♯ minor harmonic, from Subdominant to Subdominant
c) E minor harmonic, from Dominant to Dominant
d) B♭ minor melodic, from Tonic to Tonic
e) F♯ minor harmonic, from Subdominant to Subdominant

7. Write these scales ascending and descending, in the bass clef, using the correct key-signature for each.

a) the melodic minor scale whose Supertonic is D

b) the harmonic minor scale whose Dominant is B♭

c) the melodic minor scale whose Leading-note is G♯

d) the harmonic minor scale whose Subdominant is E♭

e) the harmonic minor scale whose Mediant is A

8. Add the proper clef, key-signature, and accidentals where necessary, to the following so as to form these scales.

a) G♭ major

b) E major

c) G minor melodic

d) E♭ major

e) E minor harmonic

f) G♯ minor harmonic

C STILL MORE EXERCISES (p. 43)

1. Write these scales in the alto clef, ascending and descending, using the correct key-signature for each.

a) A♭ minor harmonic

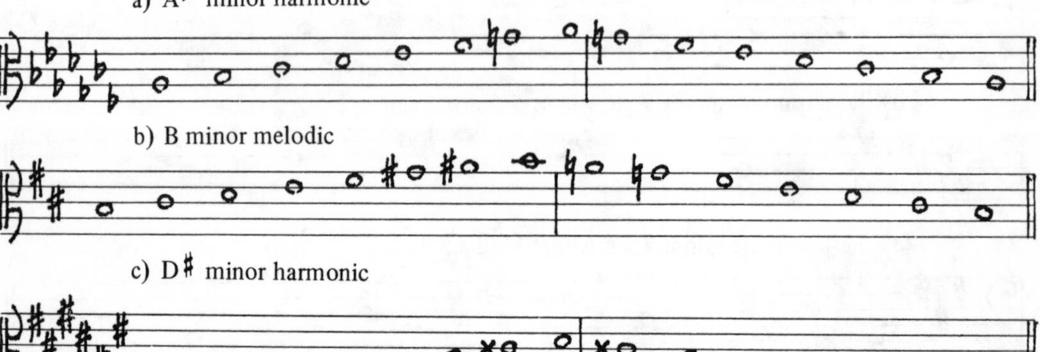

b) B minor melodic

c) D♯ minor harmonic

d) G minor harmonic

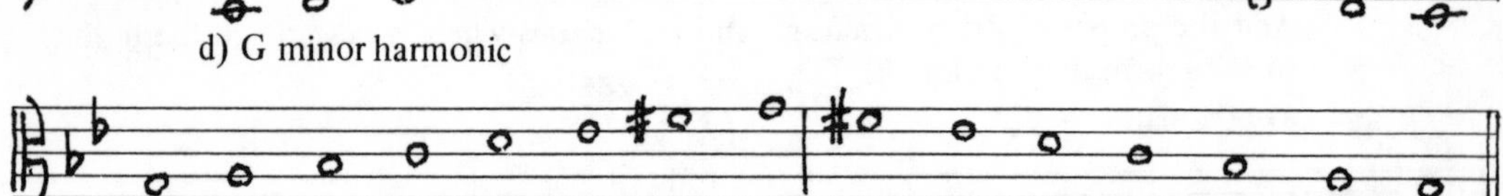

2. Write these scales in the tenor clef, ascending and descending, using the correct key-signature for each.

a) C minor melodic

b) G♯ minor harmonic

c) E minor melodic

d) F♯ minor melodic

3. Write these scales in the alto clef ascending and descending, using accidentals instead of a key signature.

a) C minor harmonic

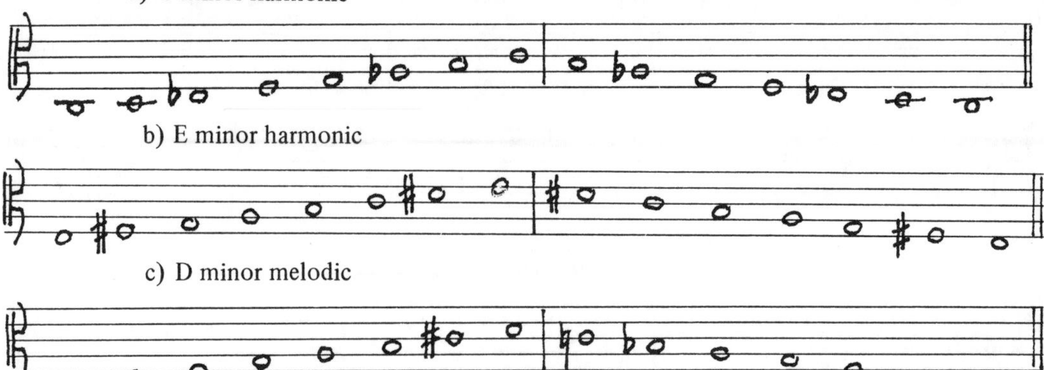

d) F♯ minor harmonic

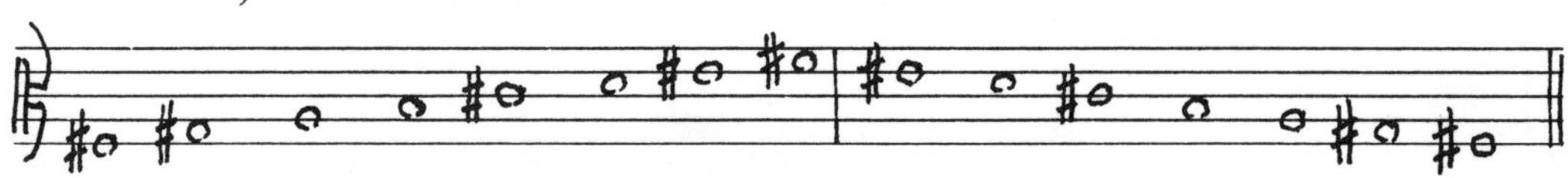

4. Write these scales in the tenor clef ascending and descending, using accidentals instead of a key signature.

a) B minor harmonic

b) E♭ minor harmonic

c) A♭ minor melodic

d) C♯ minor harmonic

5. Write these scales in the alto clef, ascending and descending, using the correct key signature for each.

a) A minor melodic from Subdominant to Subdominant

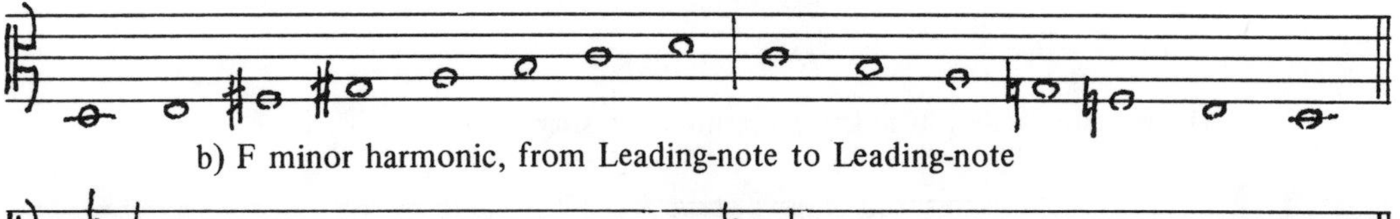

b) F minor harmonic, from Leading-note to Leading-note

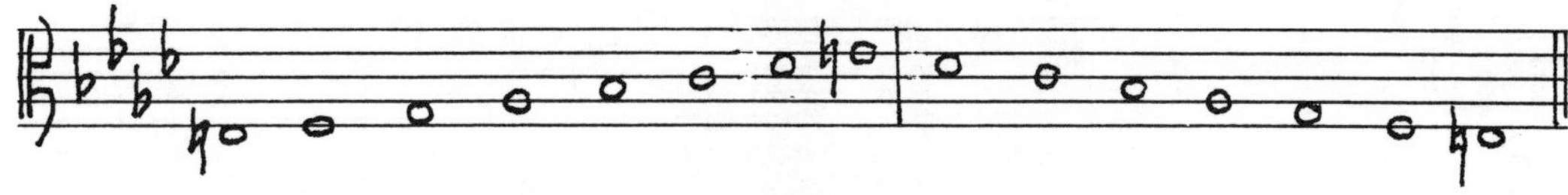

c) G♯ minor harmonic, from Mediant to Mediant

d) B minor harmonic, from Leading-note to Leading-note

e) C minor melodic, from Supertonic to Supertonic

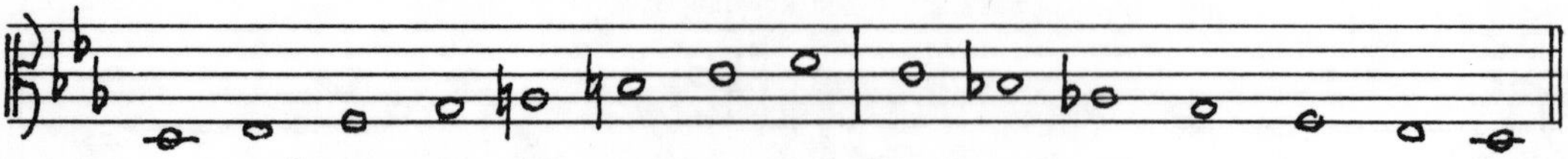

f) E♭ minor harmonic, from Submediant to Submediant

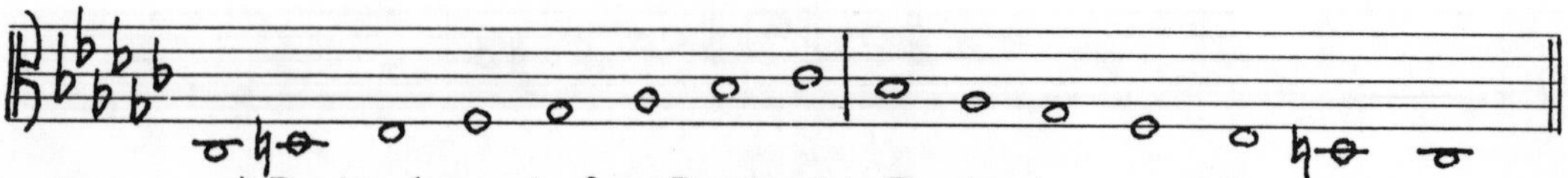

g) D minor harmonic, from Dominant to Dominant

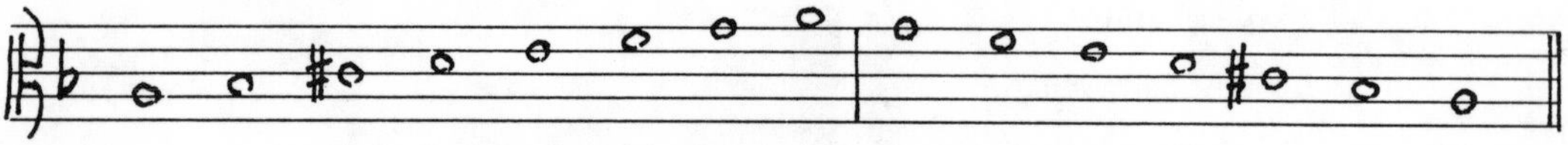

h) F♯ minor melodic from Supertonic to Supertonic.

i) B♭ minor harmonic from Subdominant to Subdominant

j) A♯ minor melodic, from Dominant to Dominant

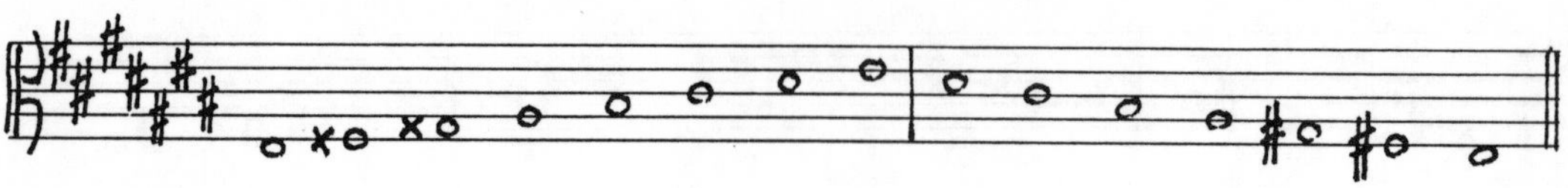

6. Write these scales in the tenor clef, ascending and descending, using the correct key-signature for each.

a) the major scale whose key signature is six sharps

b) its relative minor, harmonic

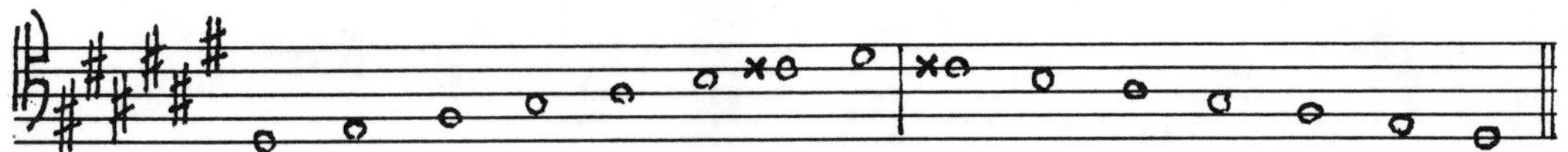

c) its tonic minor, melodic

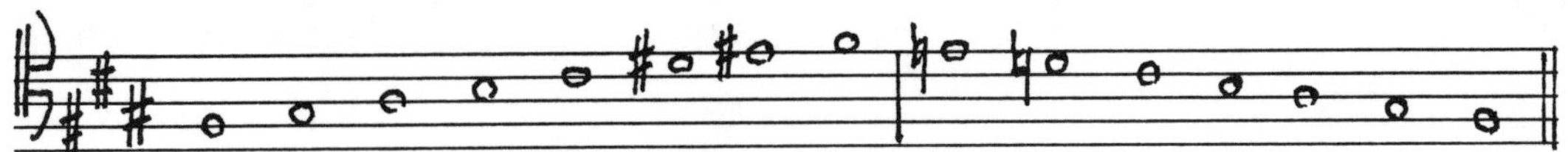

7. Write these scales in the bass clef, ascending and descending, using the correct key-signature for each.

The harmonic minor scale whose key signature is four sharps

b) its relative major

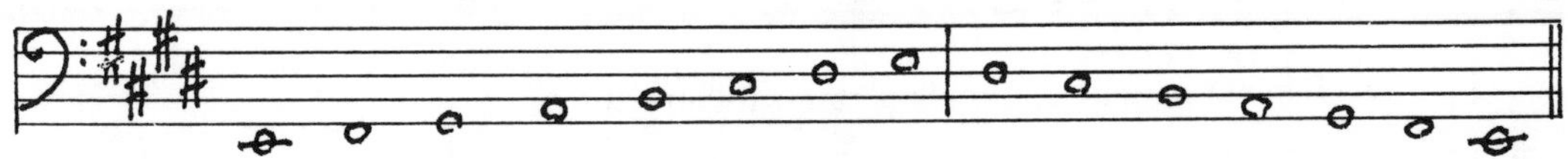

c) its tonic major

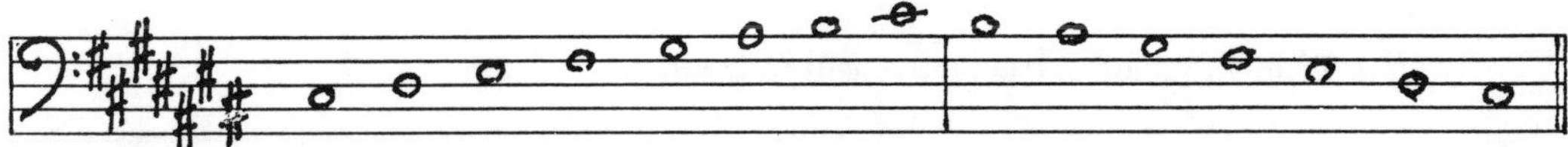

8. Add the proper clef, key signature, and accidentals where necessary to the following so as to form these scales.

a) D major, from Mediant to Mediant

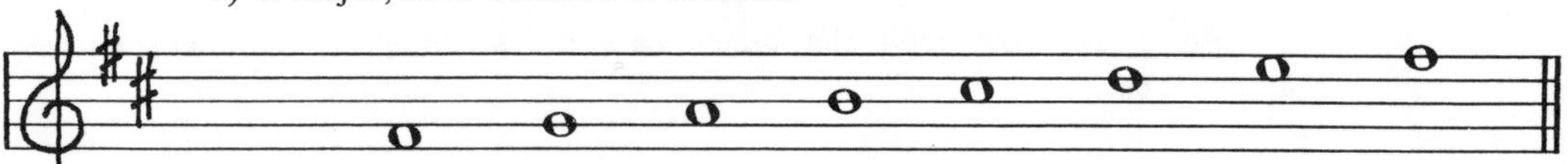

b) G minor melodic, from Submediant to Submediant

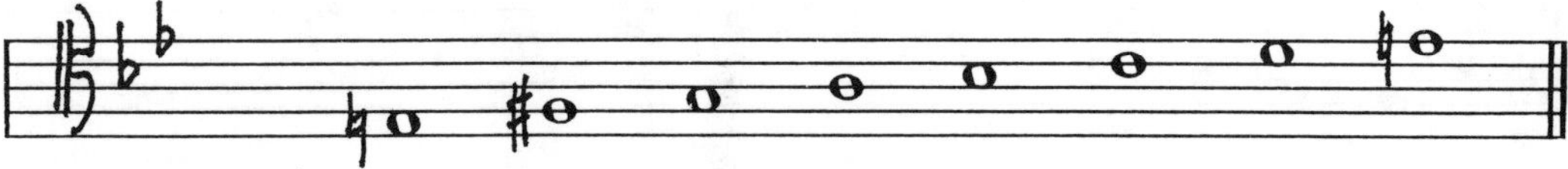

c) C♯ major, from Submediant to Submediant

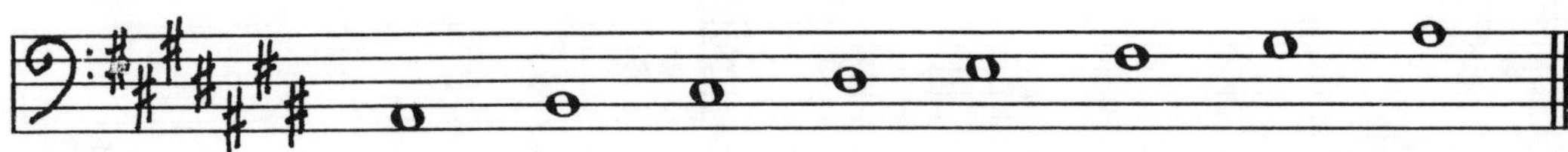

d) F♯ minor harmonic, from Tonic to Tonic

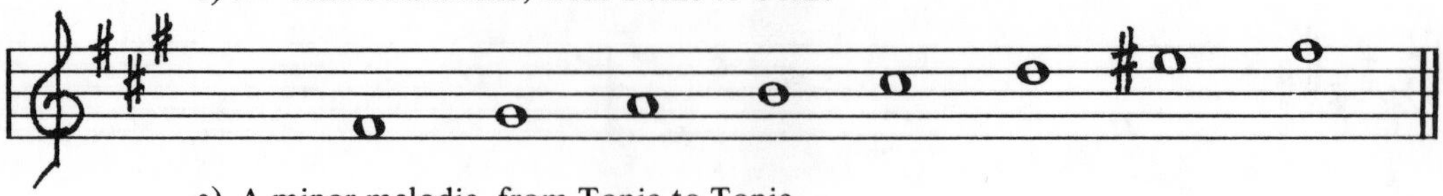

e) A minor melodic, from Tonic to Tonic

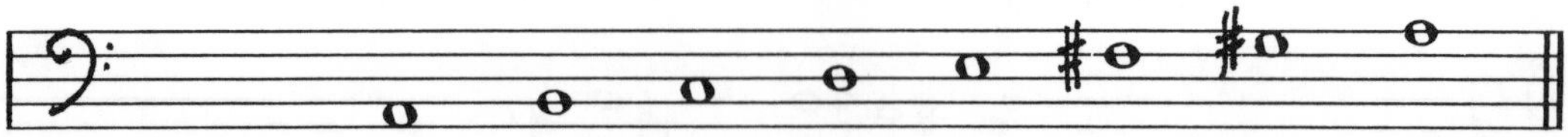

f) E minor melodic from Mediant to Mediant

g) B♭ major, from Dominant to Dominant

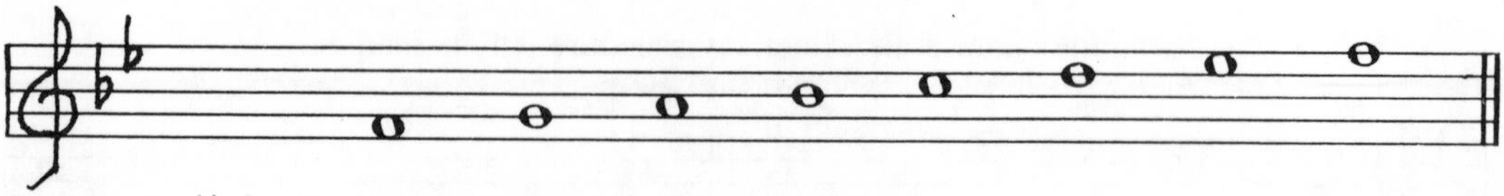

h) C minor harmonic, from Mediant to Mediant

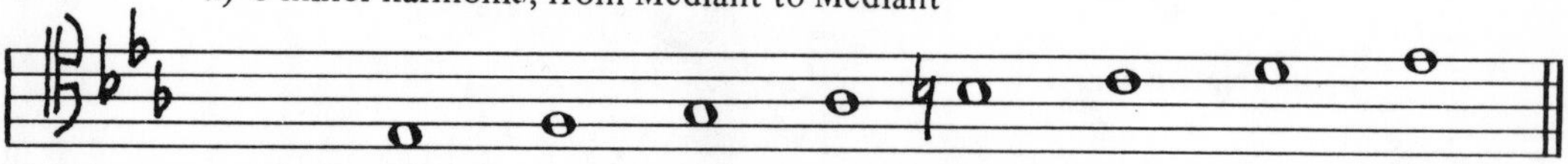

i) F minor harmonic, from Supertonic to Supertonic

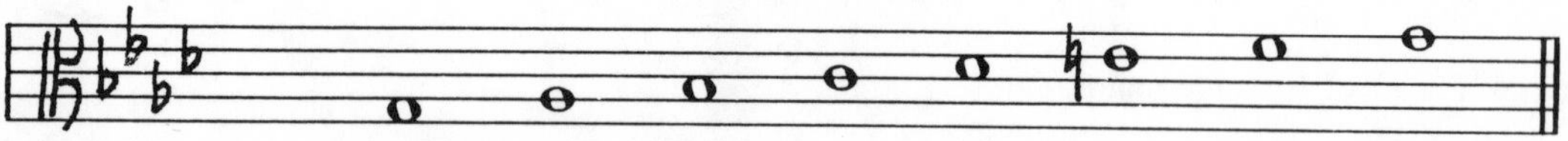

j) D minor melodic, from Dominant to Dominant

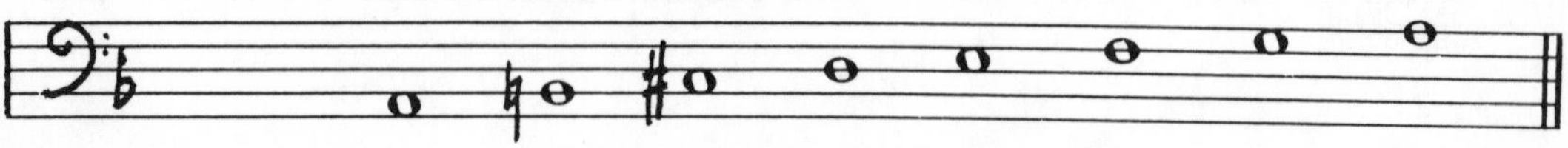

9. Write these scales in the treble clef, ascending and descending, using the correct key-signature for each.

a) E♭ major

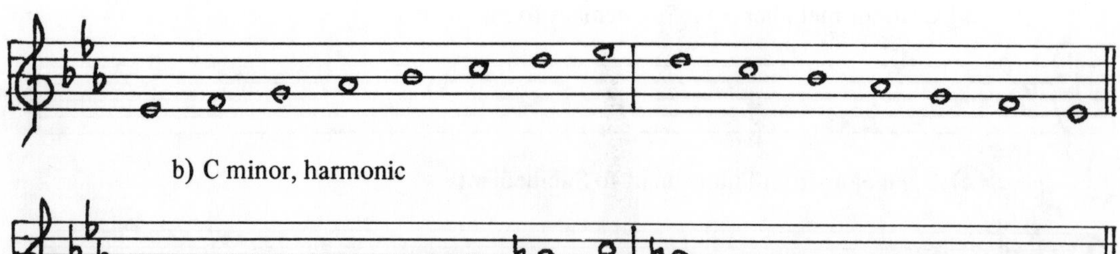

b) C minor, harmonic

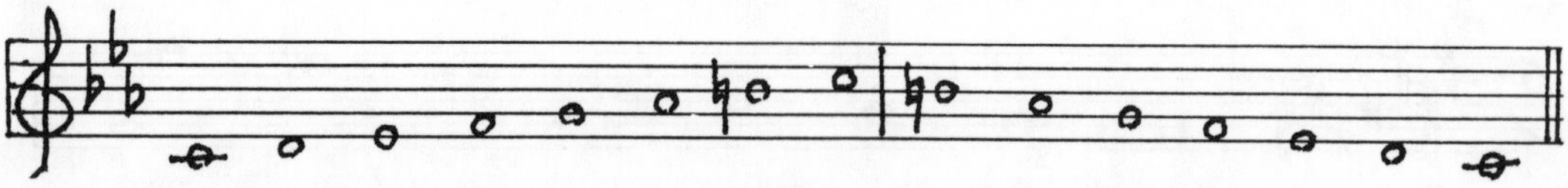

c) E♭ minor, melodic

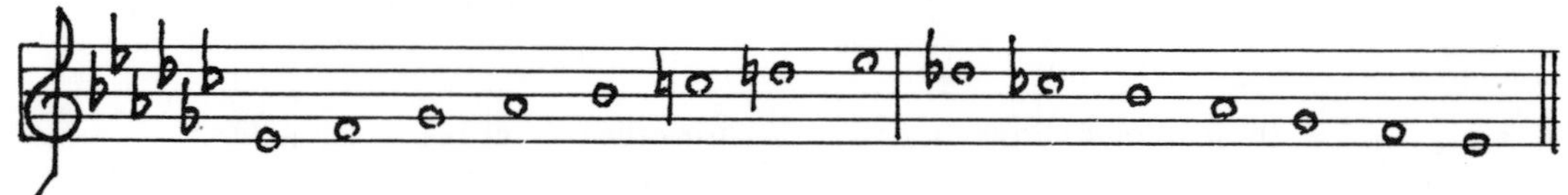

d) D♯ minor, harmonic

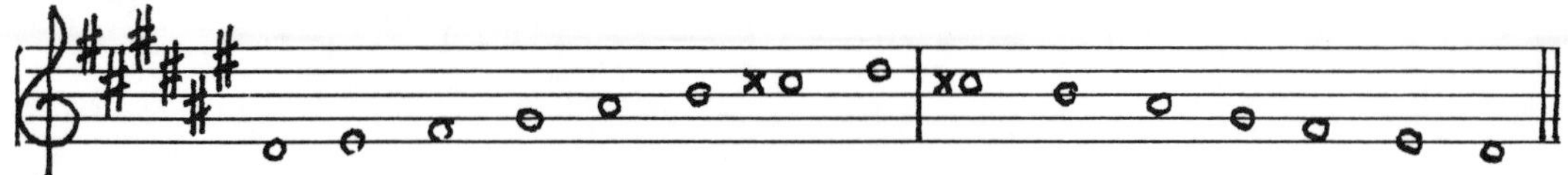

State the relationship of the first scale in question 9 to each of the last three.

relationship of a) to b) a) is relative major to b)

relationship of a) to c) a) is tonic major to c)

relationship of a) to d) a) is enharmonic tonic major to d)

C EXERCISES (p. 49)

1. Write these scales in the treble clef.

a) the harmonic chromatic scale of G, without using a key signature

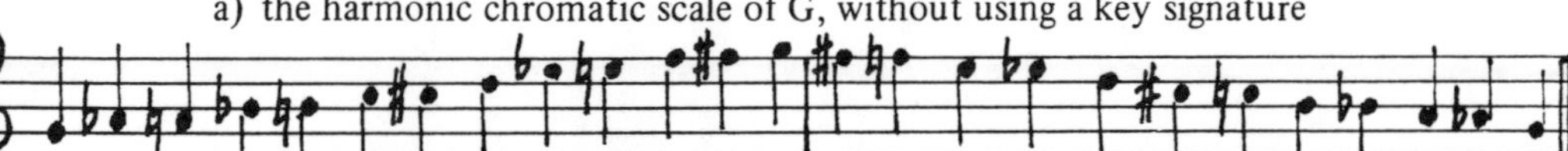

b) the harmonic chromatic scale of F, using the correct key signature.

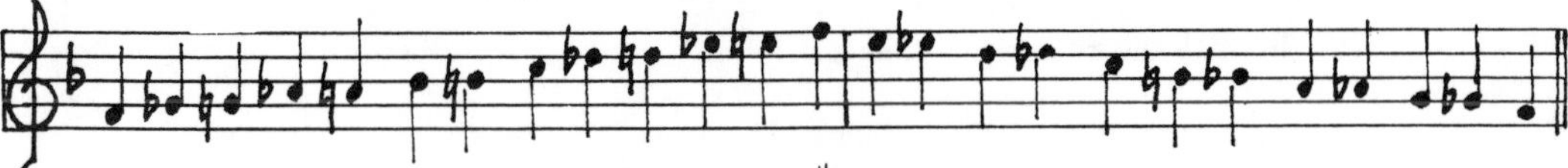

c) the melodic chromatic scale of F♯.

2. Write these scales in the tenor clef.

a) the melodic chromatic scale of A♭ .

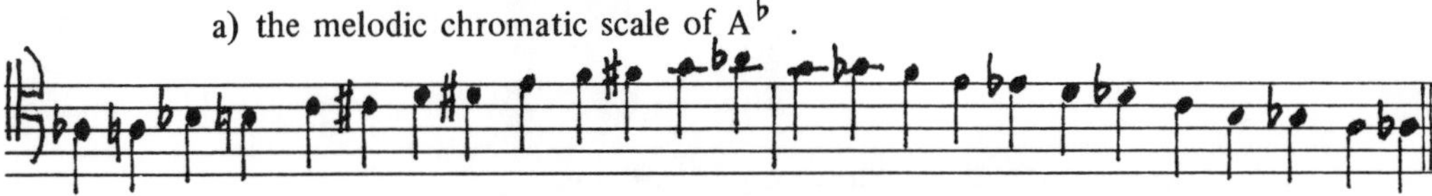

b) the harmonic chromatic scale of E, using the correct key signature.

c) the harmonic chromatic scale of B, without using a key signature.

3. Write these scales in the bass clef.

a) the harmonic chromatic scale of A, using the correct key signature.

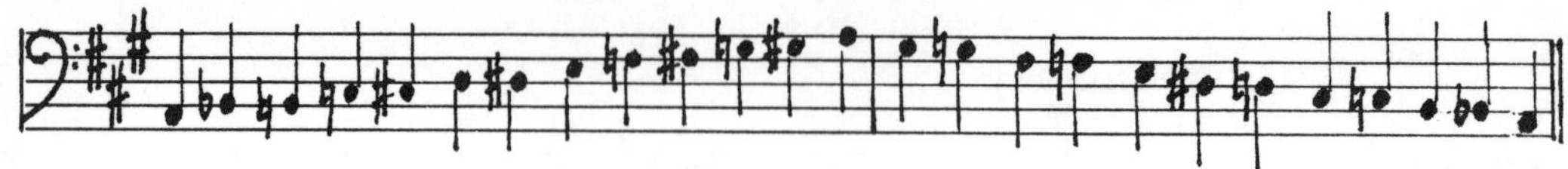

b) the melodic chromatic scale of C♯.

c) the harmonic chromatic scale of E♭, without using a key signature.

4. Write these scales in the alto clef.

a) the melodic chromatic scale of F.

b) the harmonic chromatic scale of C.

c) the harmonic chromatic scale of B♭ , using the correct key signature.

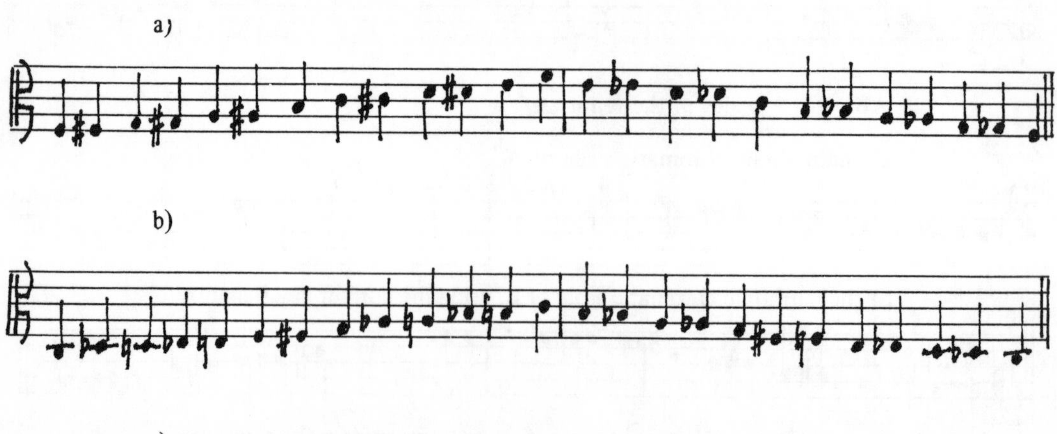

A B C EXERCISES (p. 55)

1. Name the following intervals. Use abbreviations + for major, – for minor and P for perfect.

−3
−6
+3
P5
+2
+6
+7
P4
P8
−7

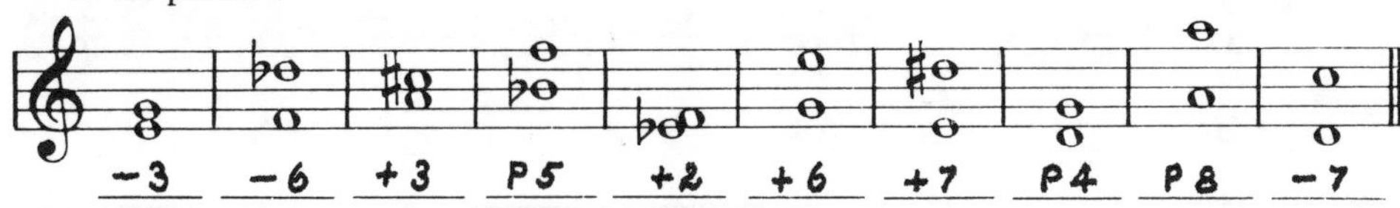

2. Write ALL of the following intervals above EACH given note.

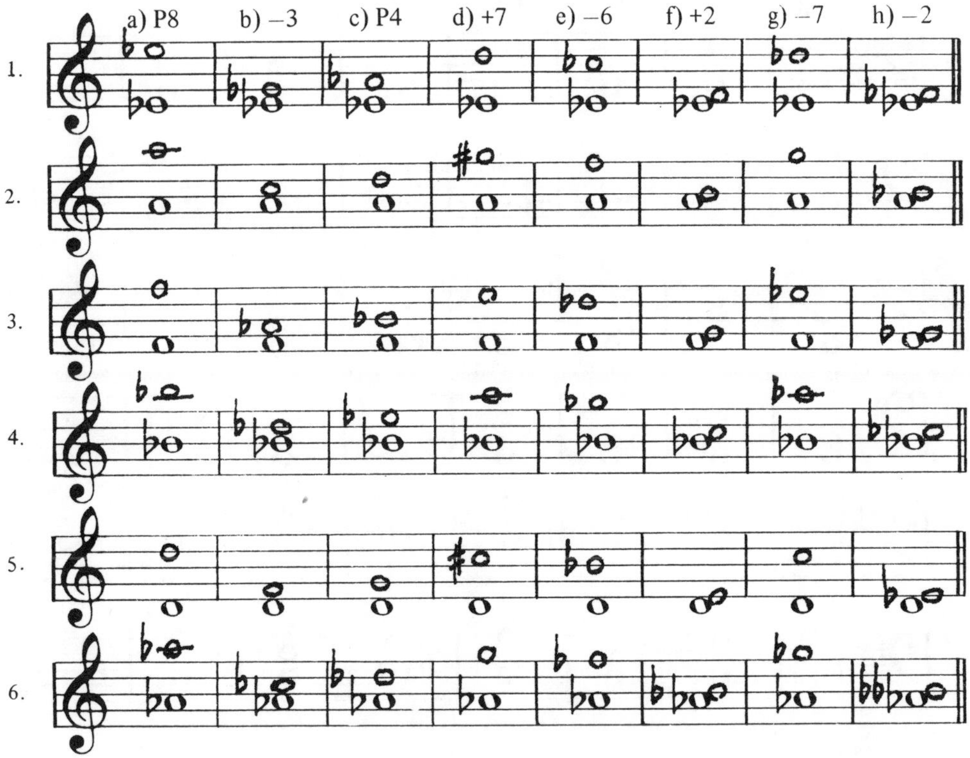

a) P8
b) –3
c) P4
d) +7
e) –6
f) +2
g) –7
h) –2
1.
2.
3.
4.
5.
6.

3. Name the following intervals.

+3
P5
−6
−2
+7

P4
−3
+6
+2
+7

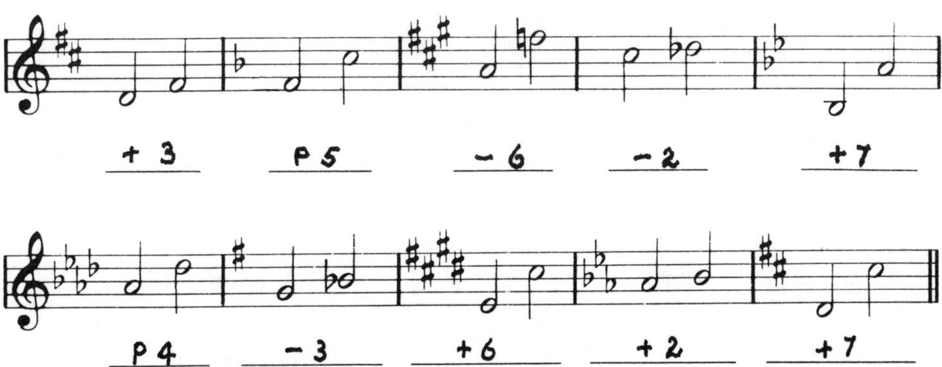

4. Name the following intervals.

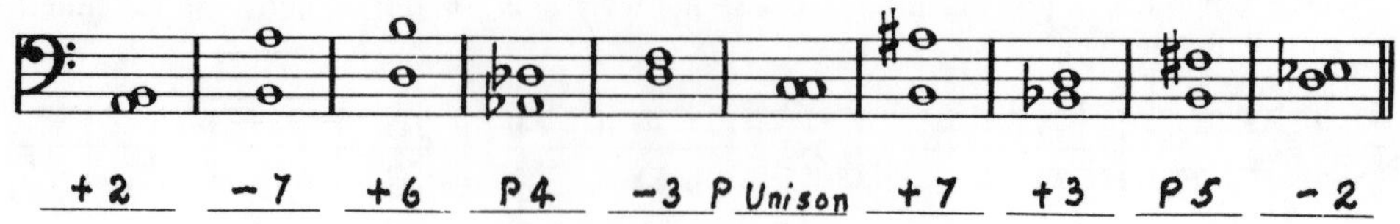

5. Write ALL of these intervals above EACH given note.

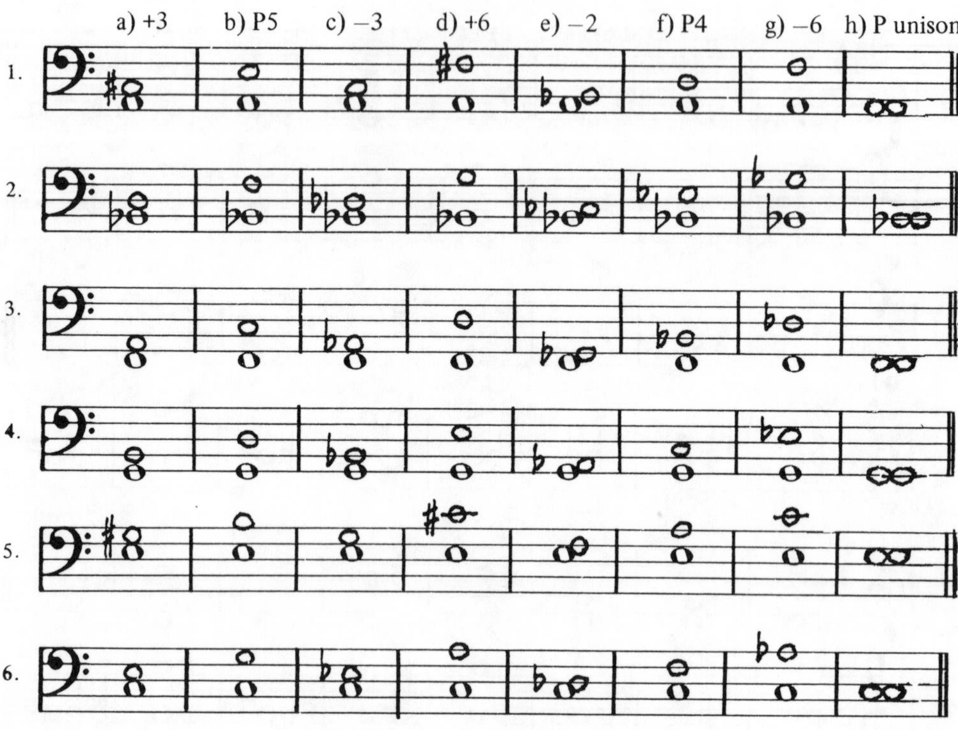

6. Name the following intervals.

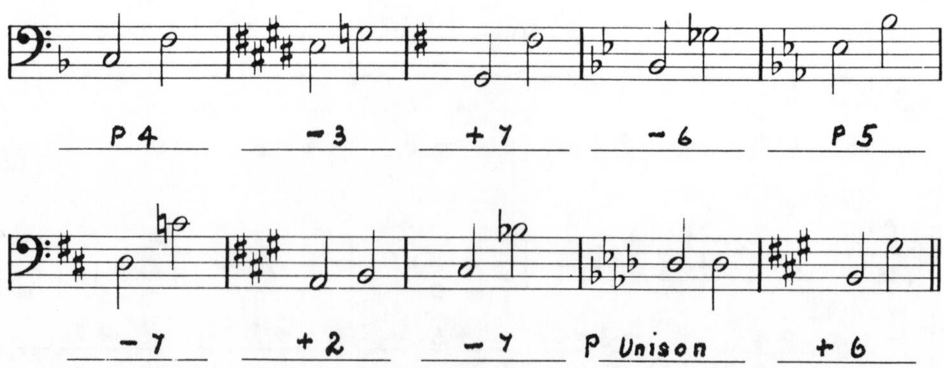

B C EXERCISES (p. 58)

1. Name these intervals. Invert them on the staff directly underneath and re-name them.

3. Write the following intervals above the given notes. Invert and re-name them.

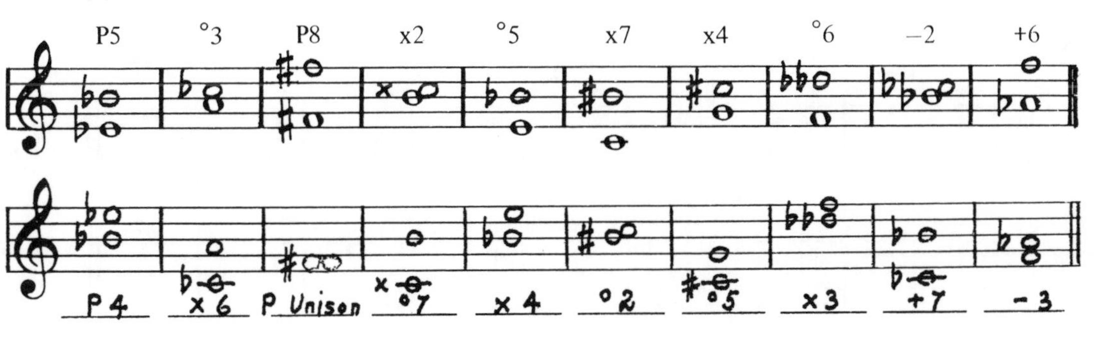

4. Write ALL of these intervals above EACH of these notes.

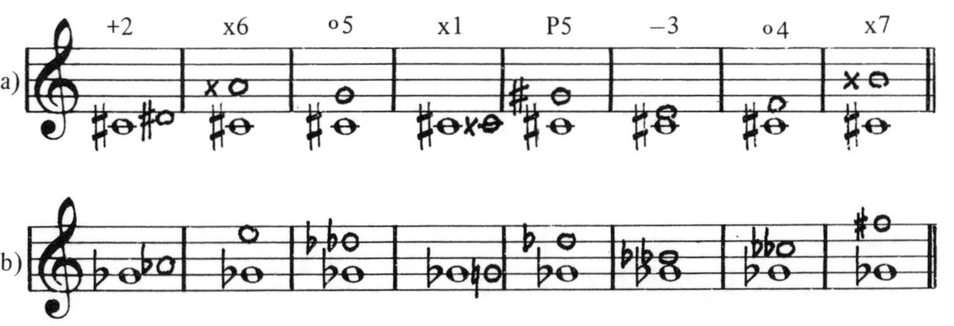

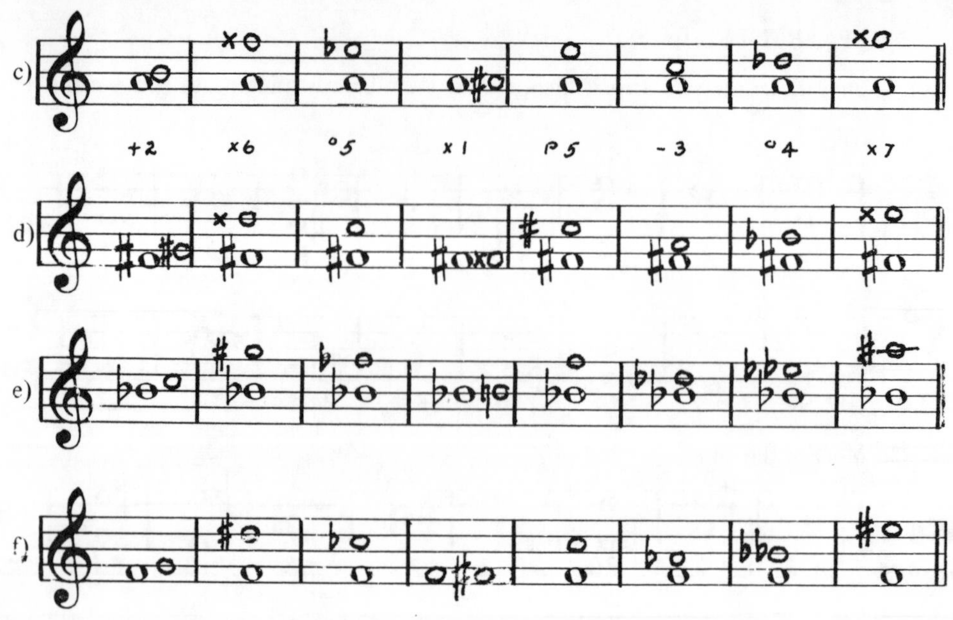

5. Write ALL of these intervals above EACH of these notes.

+6 x2 °3 –7 x5 °4 –2 P8

a)

b)

c)

d)

e)

f)

C EXERCISES (p. 61)

1. Name these intervals.

2. Name these intervals. Invert them in the tenor clef, and re-name them.

3. Name these intervals.

4. Name these intervals.

5. Write ALL these intervals below EACH of the given notes.

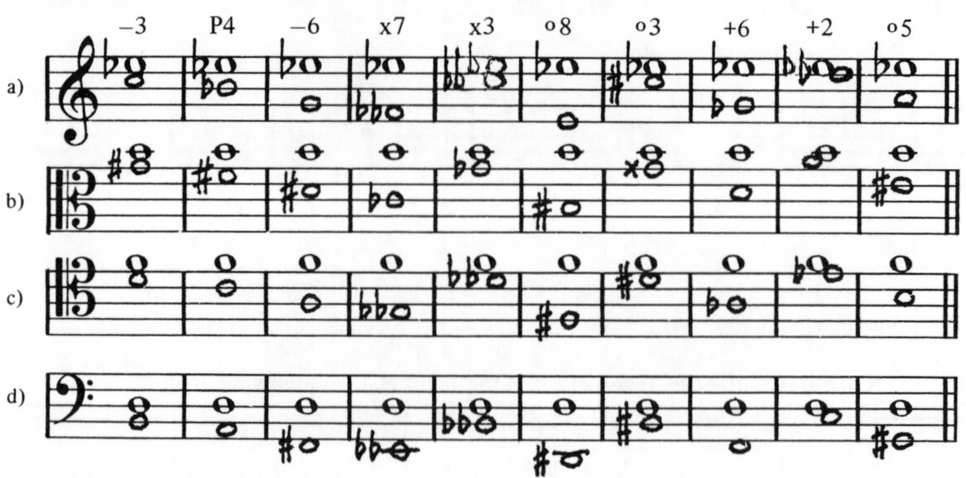

6. Write ALL these intervals above EACH of the given notes.

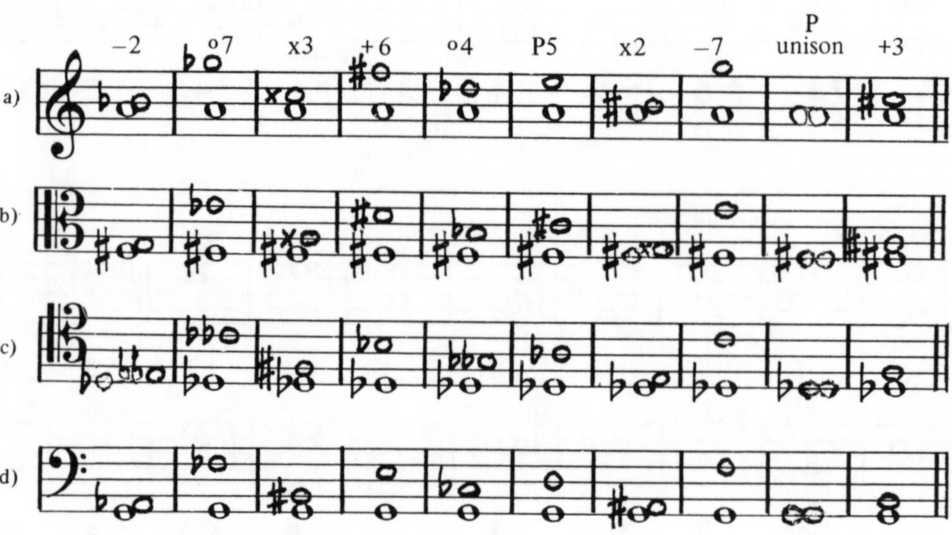

7. Name these intervals. Change the upper note of each enharmonically and re-name.

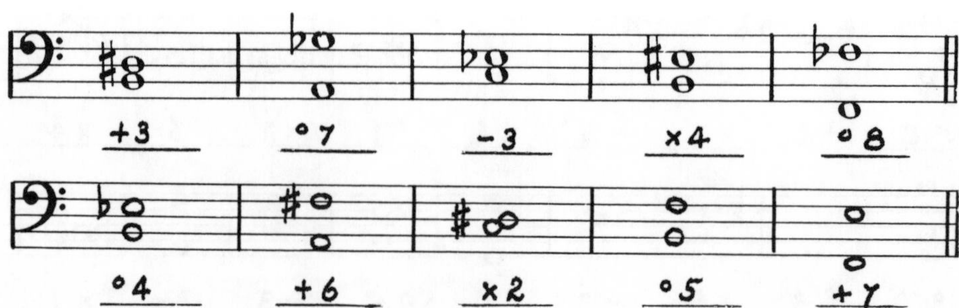

8. Name these intervals. Change the lower note of each enharmonically and re-name.

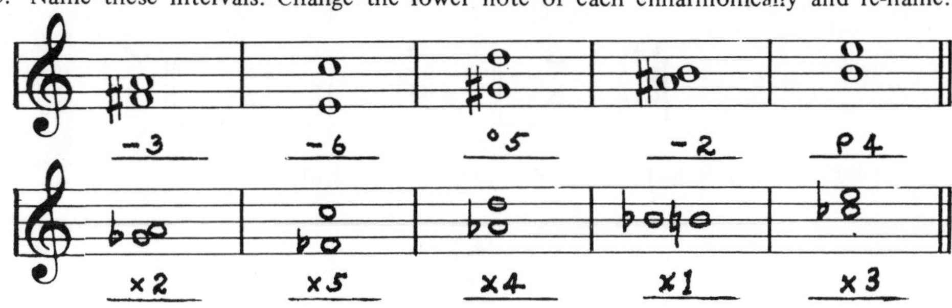

9. Name these compound intervals. Invert them and re-name.

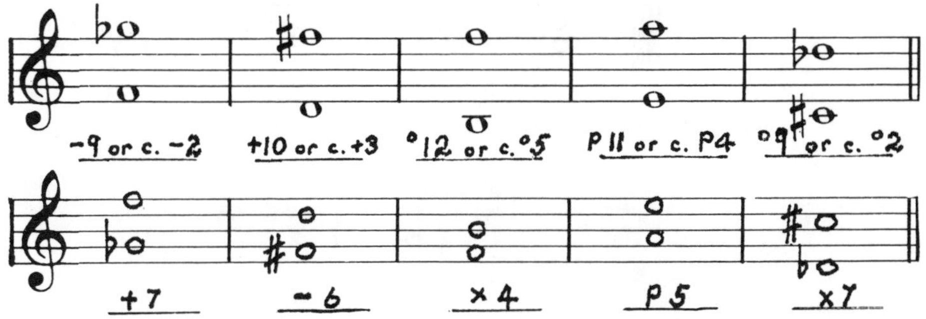

10. Name the intervals between successive notes of the following.

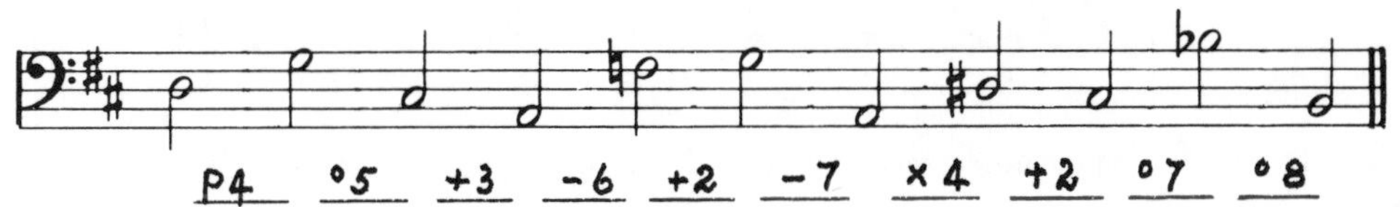

11. Name all the keys in which each of these intervals may be found.

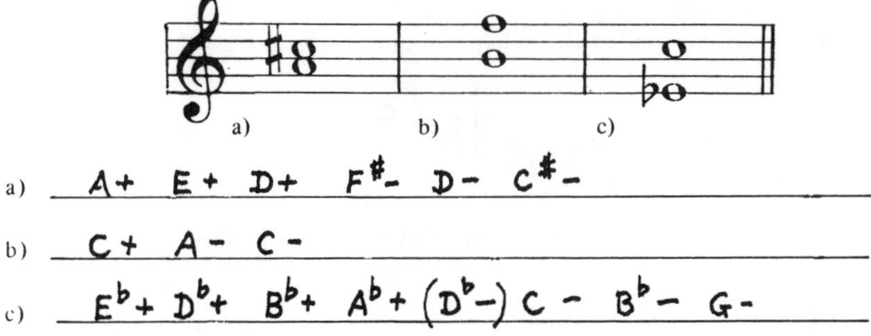

12. Write three different major thirds that are found in the key of E♭ major.

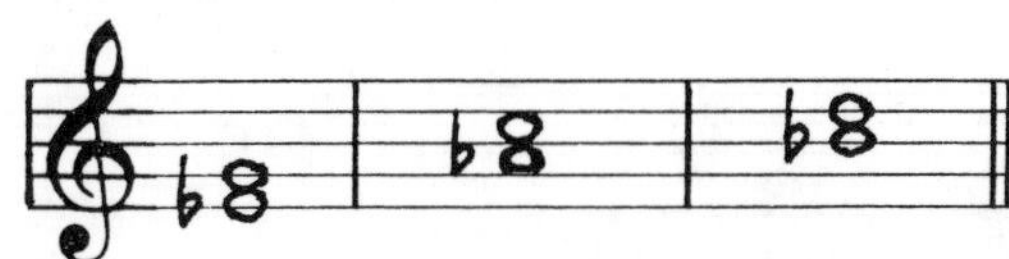

13. Write three different major sixths that are found in the key of F minor.

14. Write a diminished seventh that is found in the key of G minor.

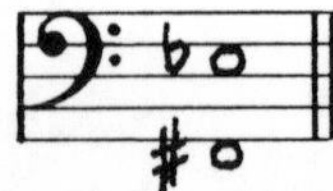

15. Write three different perfect fourths that are found in the key of B major.

16. Write three different minor seconds that are found in the key of C♯ minor.

17. Write four different major seconds that are found in the key of A major.

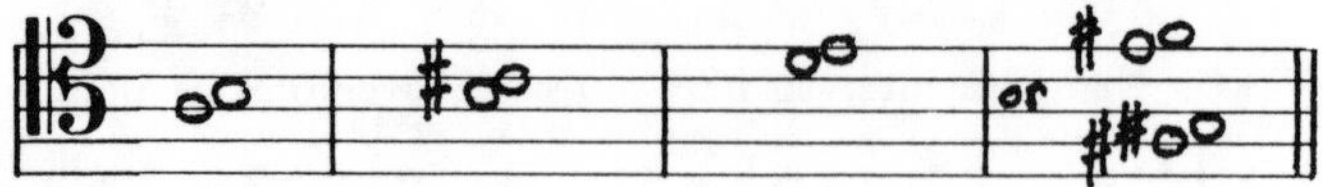

18. Write an augmented second that is found in the key of G♯ minor.

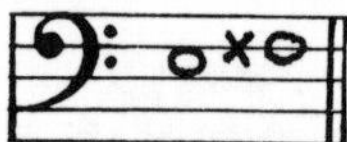

19. Write the augmented fifth that is found in the key of B minor.

20. Write four different minor thirds that are found in the key of E major.

21. Mark three major thirds between the different notes of this scale.

22. Name this interval. Invert it in the tenor clef, and re-name it.

Name all the keys in which the above interval may be found.

A♭+ D♭+ G♭+ C♭+ A♭– (D♭–) (G♭–) F –

23. Name all the keys in which each of these intervals may be found.

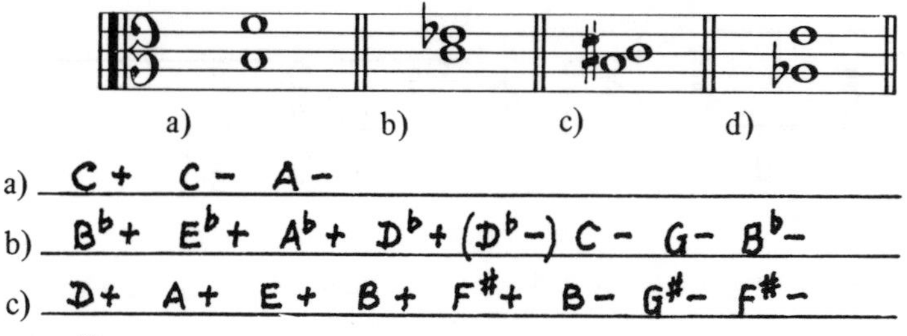

24. Mark all the perfect fourths that occur between the different notes of this scale.

25. Name the following intervals. Name the one key that contains them all.

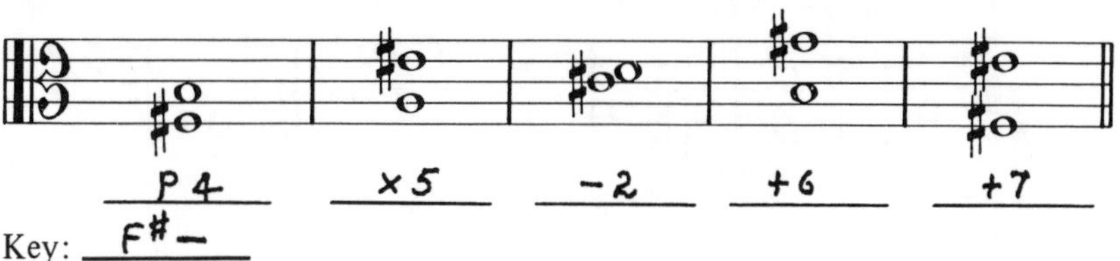

A B C EXERCISES (p. 66)

1. Write these triads in the treble clef, using the correct key signature for each.

a) the Dominant triad of A major
b) the Tonic triad of F major
c) the Dominant triad of E♭ major
d) the Tonic triad of G major
e) the Dominant triad of E major
f) the Tonic triad of D major
g) the Tonic triad of C major

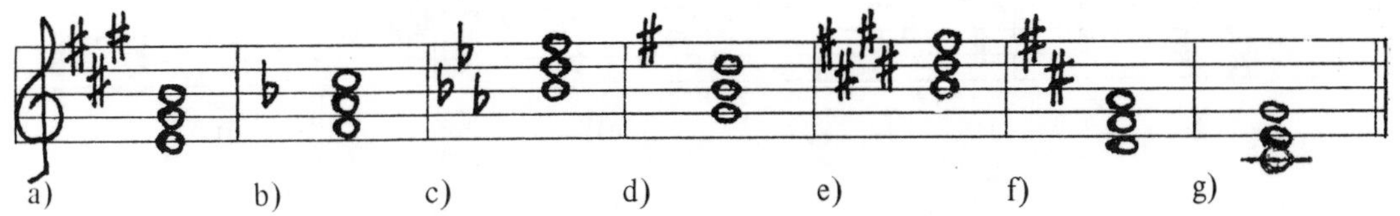

2. Write these triads in the bass clef, using accidentals instead of a key signature.

a) the Tonic triad of A♭ major
b) the Dominant triad of C major
c) the Tonic triad of B♭ major
d) the Dominant triad of D major
e) the Tonic triad of E♭ major
f) the Tonic triad of A major
g) the Dominant triad of G major
h) the Tonic triad of E major
i) the Dominant triad of F major.

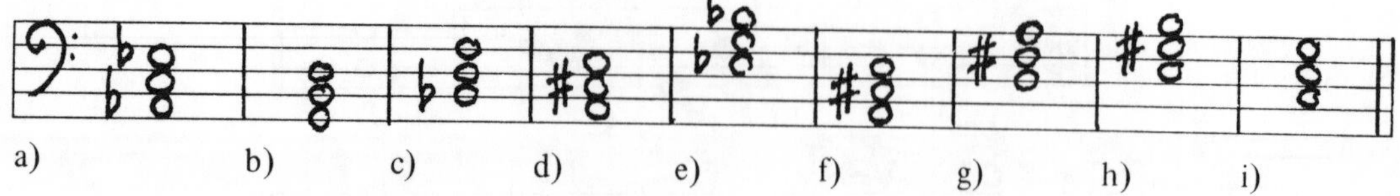

3. Write these triads in the treble clef, using accidentals instead of a key signature.

a) the Tonic triad of B minor
b) the Dominant triad of C♯ minor
c) the Tonic triad of F♯ minor
d) the Dominant triad of G minor
e) the Tonic triad of A minor
f) the Dominant triad of D minor
g) the Tonic triad of C minor
h) the Dominant triad of E minor
i) the Tonic triad of F minor

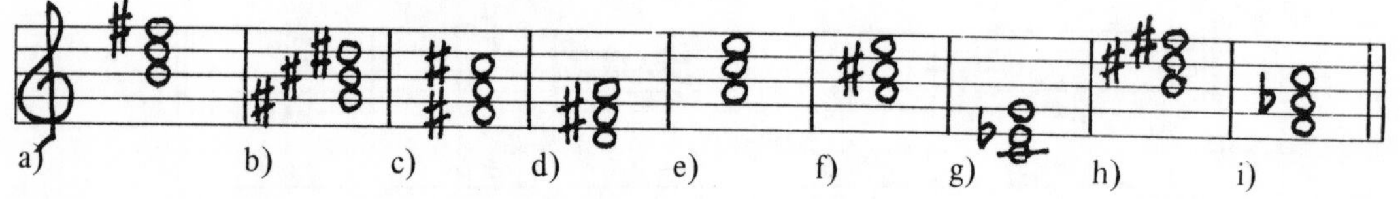

4. Write these triads in the bass clef, using the correct key signature for each.

a) the Dominant triad of C minor
b) the Tonic triad of D minor
c) the Dominant triad of F♯ minor
d) the Tonic triad of E minor
e) the Dominant triad of F minor
f) the Tonic triad of C♯ minor
g) the Tonic triad of G minor

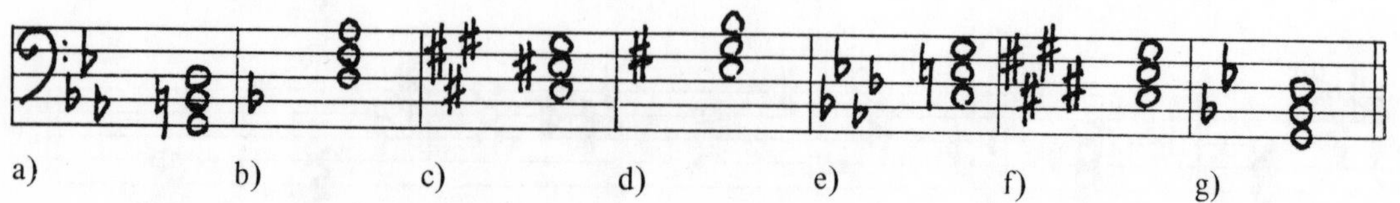

5. Fill in the blanks.

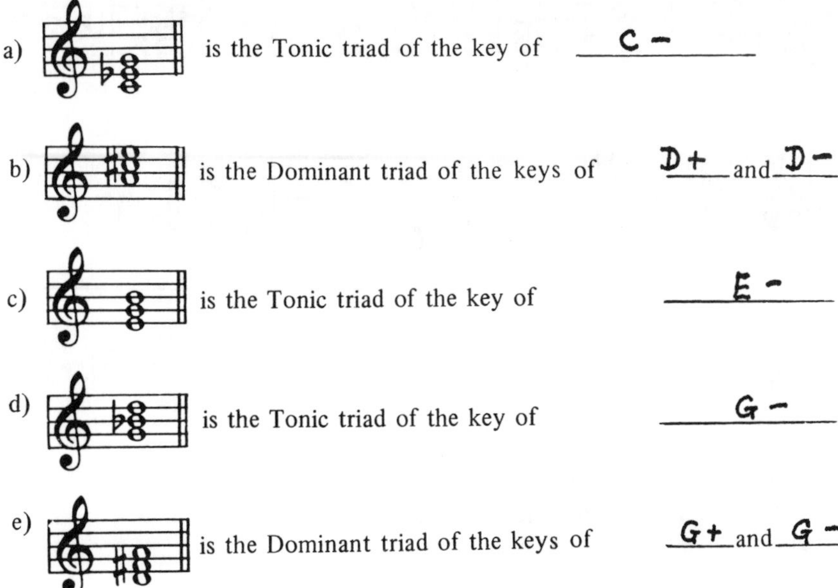

a) is the Tonic triad of the key of C −

b) is the Dominant triad of the keys of D + and D −

c) is the Tonic triad of the key of E −

d) is the Tonic triad of the key of G −

e) is the Dominant triad of the keys of G + and G −

6. Fill in the blanks.

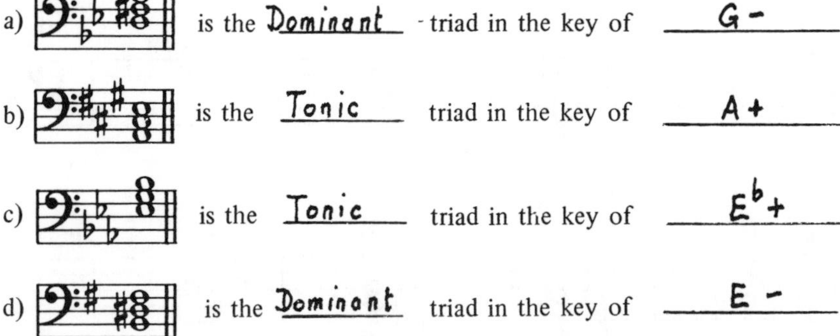

a) is the Dominant triad in the key of G −

b) is the Tonic triad in the key of A +

c) is the Tonic triad in the key of E♭ +

d) is the Dominant triad in the key of E −

B C EXERCISES (p. 69)

1. Write a major triad and its inversions on each of these notes.

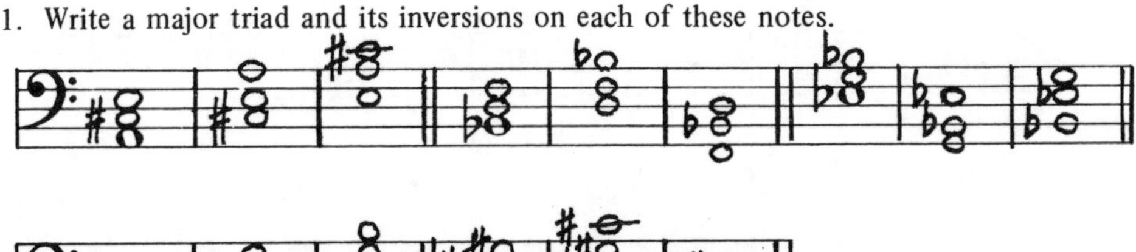

2. Write a minor triad and its inversions on each of these notes.

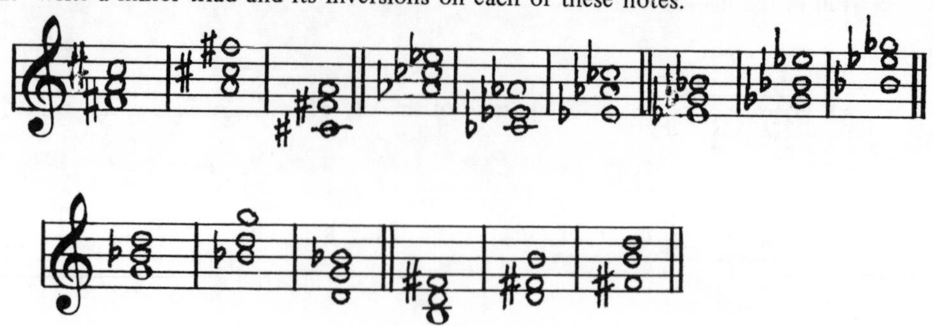

3. Write these triads in the treble clef.

a) Root position of the F major triad
b) Root position of the D minor triad
c) First inversion of the G major triad
d) Second inversion of the E minor triad
e) Root position of the B♭ minor triad
f) Second inversion of the C major triad
g) First inversion of the A♭ major triad
h) Second inversion of the G♯ minor triad
i) Root position of the B major triad
j) First inversion of the D major triad

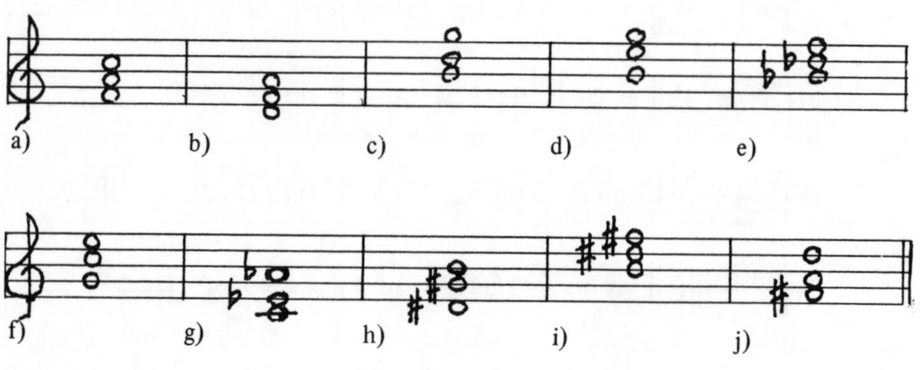

4. Solve these triads.

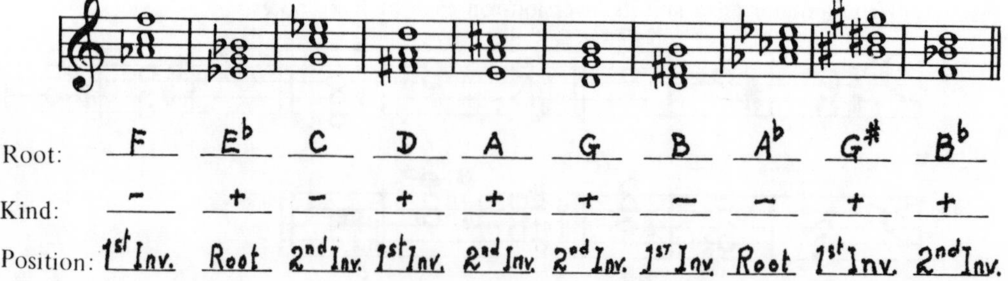

5. Write these triads in root position in the bass clef.

   a) a major triad with F as the root
   b) a minor triad with D as the fifth
   c) a minor triad with C as the third
   d) a major triad with G as the third
   e) a major triad with A♭ as the root
   f) a minor triad with A as the fifth
   g) a major triad with B as the fifth
   h) a minor triad with E♭ as the third
   i) a minor triad with B as the root
   j) a major triad with C♯ as the third

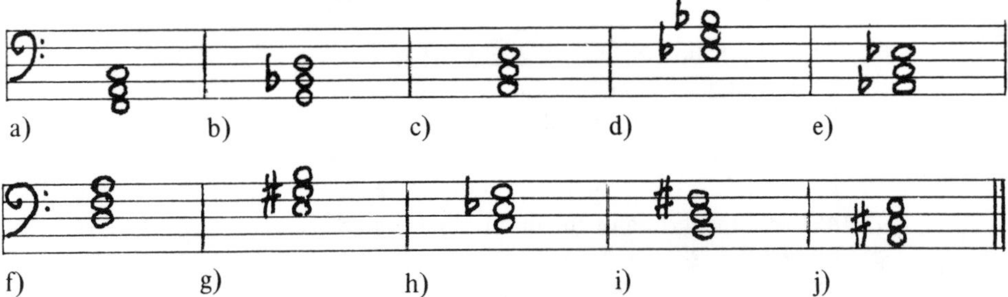

6. Add accidentals where necessary to make each of these a major triad. *

7. Add accidentals where necessary to make each of these a minor triad.

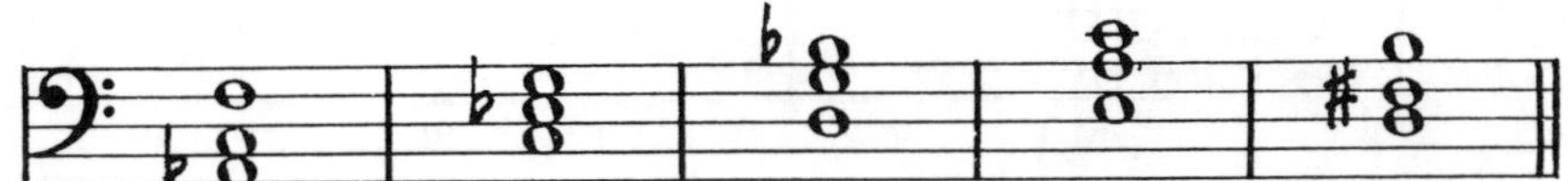

* Different accidentals than those used are also acceptable.

C EXERCISES (p. 71)

1. Solve the following triads.

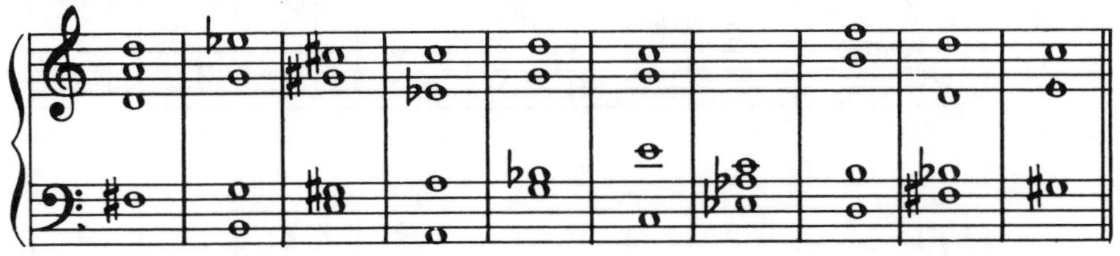

Root:	D	E♭	C♯	A	G	C	A♭	B	B♭	C
Kind:	+	×	−	o	−	+	+	o	×	×
Position:	1st	2nd	1st	Root	Root	Root	2nd	1st	2nd	2nd

2. Write these triads in close position in the treble clef.

   a) an augmented triad with D as the third
   b) a diminished triad with C♭ as the fifth
   c) a diminished triad with C♯ as the root
   d) an augmented triad with E♭ as the root
   e) an augmented triad with D as the fifth

3. Write three different arrangements of each of these triads in open position.

   a) the root position of the major triad of A♭
   b) the second inversion of the minor triad of F
   c) the first inversion of the minor triad of C
   d) the root position of the augumented triad of B
   e) the first inversion of the minor triad of F♯
   f) the second inversion of the diminished triad of E
   g) the first inversion of the augmented triad of A
   h) the root position of the diminished triad of C♯
   i) the second inversion of the major triad of D♭
   j) the first inversion of the minor triad of G

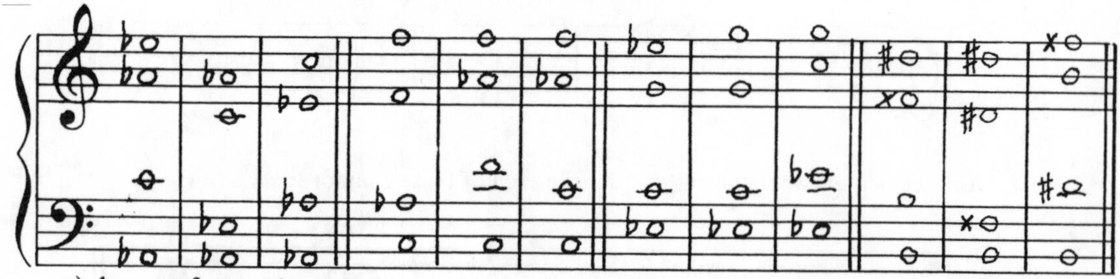

a) 1 2 3 b) 1 2 3 c) 1 2 3 d) 1 2 3

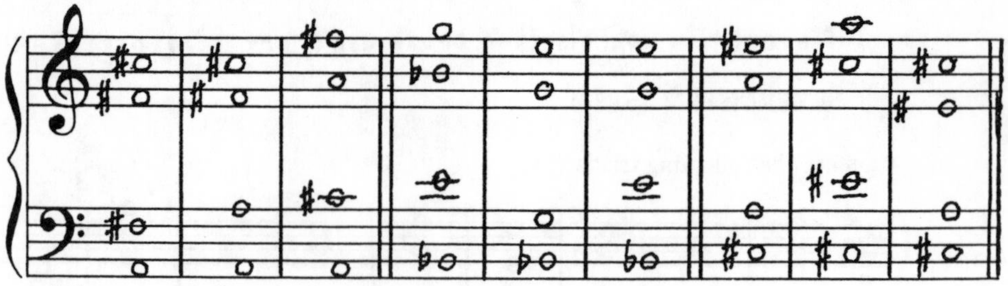

e) 1 2 3 f) 1 2 3 g) 1 2 3

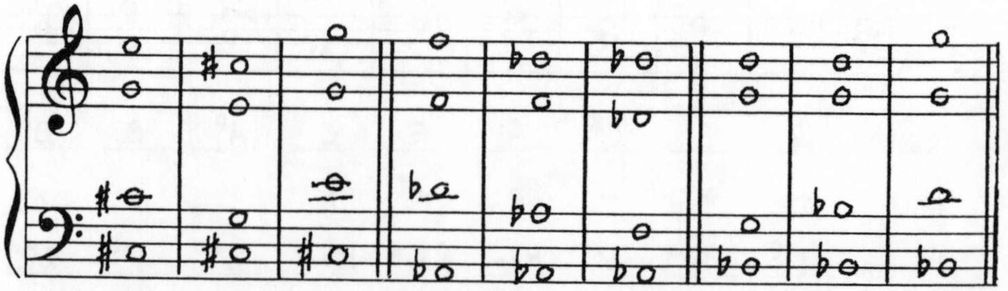

h) 1 2 3 i) 1 2 3 j) 1 2 3

Other arrangements are possible.

4. Using the proper key signature for each, write these triads in close position in the bass clef.

   a) the Supertonic triad of F major, root position.

   b) the Dominant triad of B♭ major, first inversion.

   c) the Tonic triad of F♯ minor, first inversion.

   d) the Leading-note triad of G minor, second inversion.

   e) the Mediant triad of E♭ major, root position.

   f) the Submediant triad of B major, first inversion.

   g) the Subdominant triad of C minor, second inversion.

   h) the Dominant triad of G♯ minor, root position.

   i) the Tonic triad of C♯ major, first inversion.

   j) the Supertonic triad of D minor, second inversion.

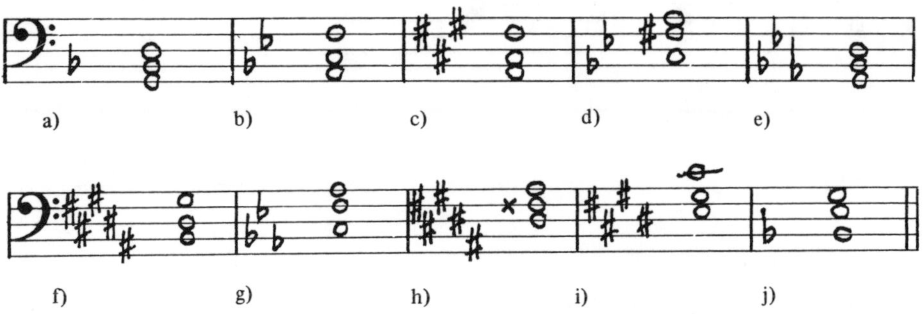

5. Write the four different kinds of triads in root position BELOW each of the following notes.

6. Write the four different kinds of triads in root position ABOVE each of the following notes.

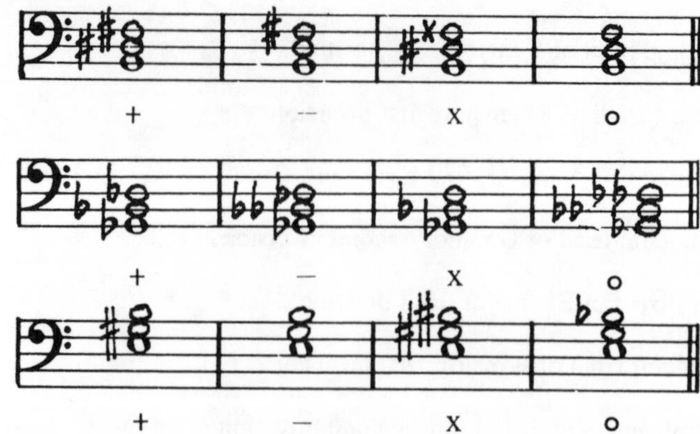

C EXERCISES (p. 75)

1. Write and name all the triads found in the key of A major.

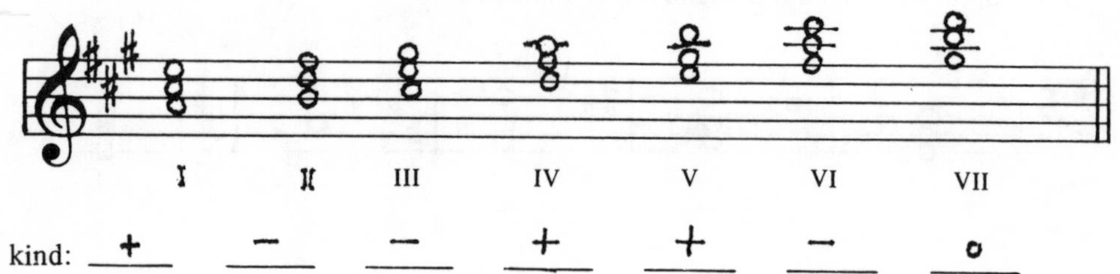

2. Write and name all the triads found in the key of E♭ major.

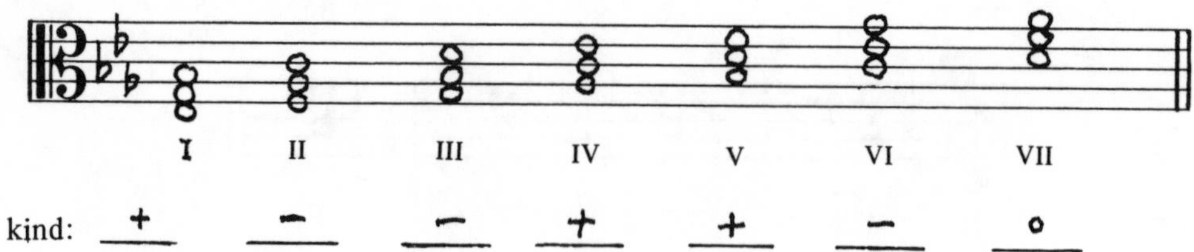

3. Write and name all the triads found in the key of F minor.

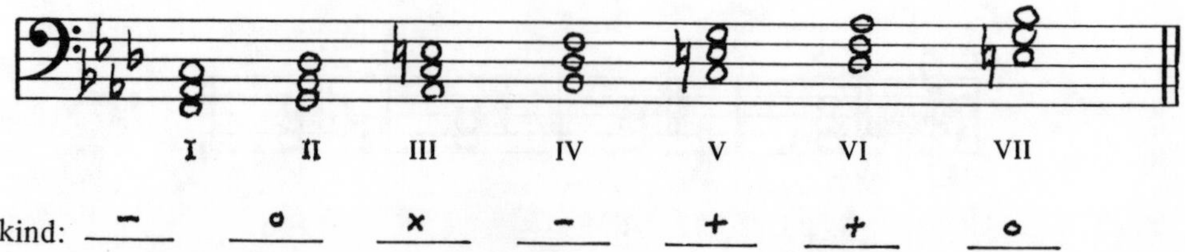

4. Write and name all the triads found in the key of G minor.

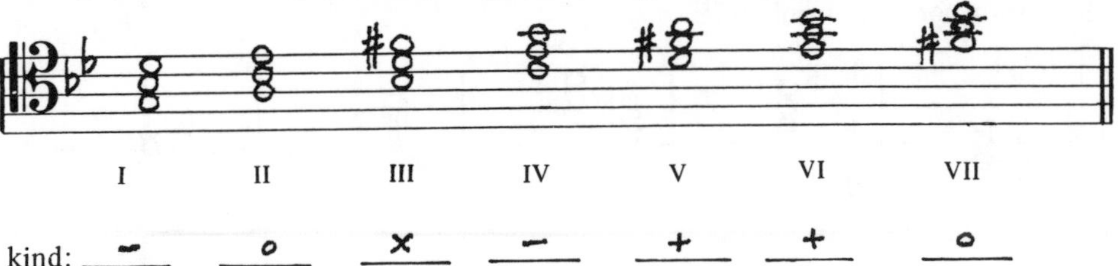

5. Name all the keys in which each of these triads is found.

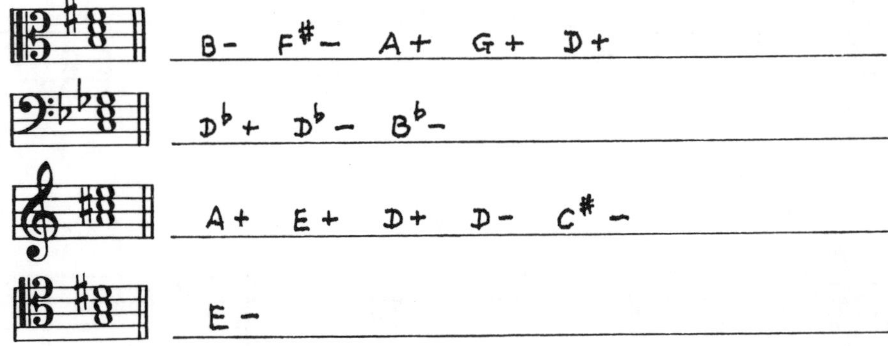

6. Write the triad that is found only in the key of G minor.

7. Write the triad that is common only to these keys: B♭ major, G minor, B♭ minor.

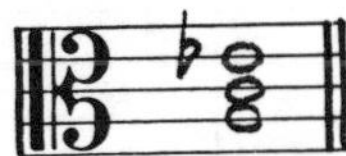

8. Name all the keys in which each of these triads is found.

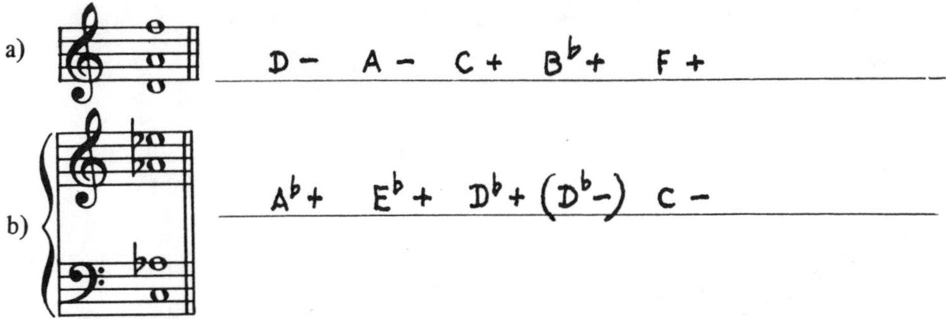

9. Write the triad that is common only to these keys: D♭ major, B♭ minor, G♭ major, F minor, and A♭ major.

10. In the treble clef, write the diminished triads that are found in a) D major, b) A♭ major c) B major d) E major e) D♭ major.

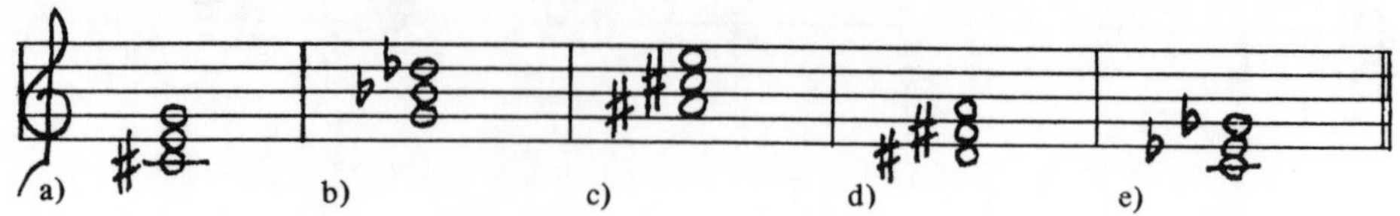

11. In the bass clef, write the augmented triads that are found in a) B minor b) G♯ minor c) C minor, d) F minor, e) D minor.

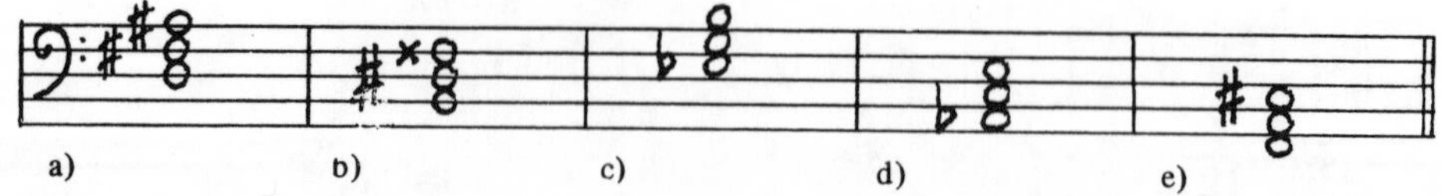

B C EXERCISES (p. 78)

1. Identify the key, and the kind of cadence for each of the following.

2. Write in 3/4 time, a two-bar example of a perfect cadence in each of these keys.
a) G major b) D♭ major c) A major d) C minor e) F minor

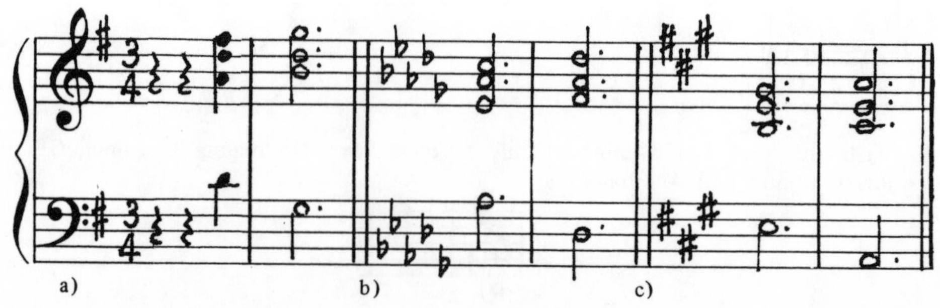

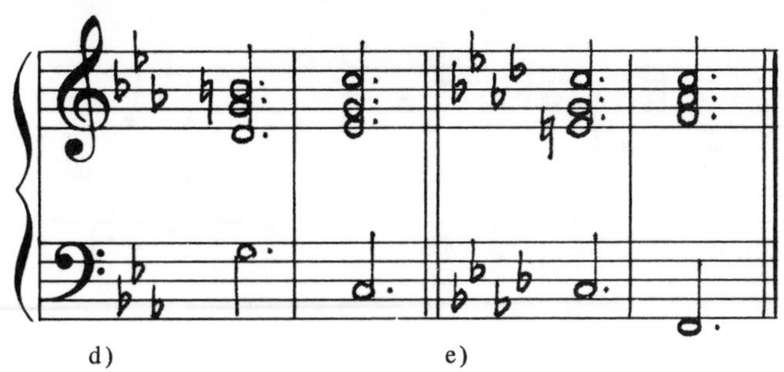

d) e)

3. Write in 2/2 time, a two-bar example of a plagal cadence in each of these keys.
   a) A♭ major b) B major c) F♯ minor d) E minor e) E major

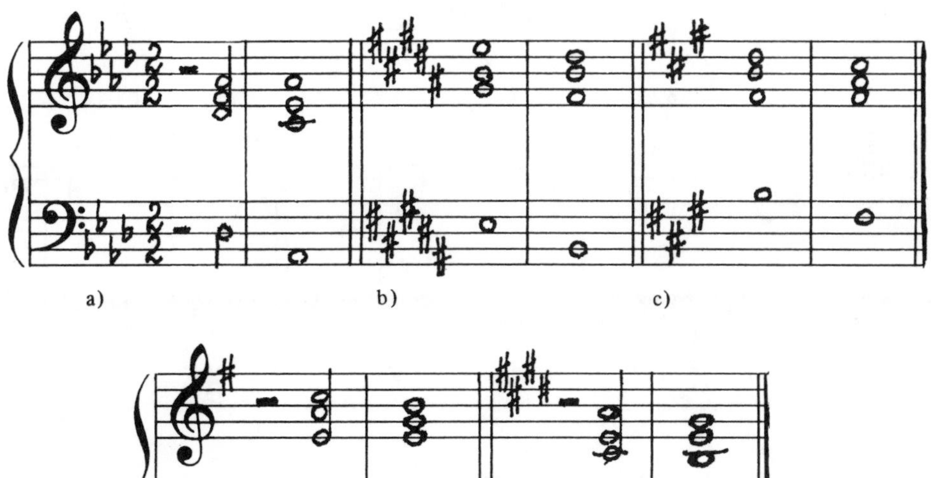

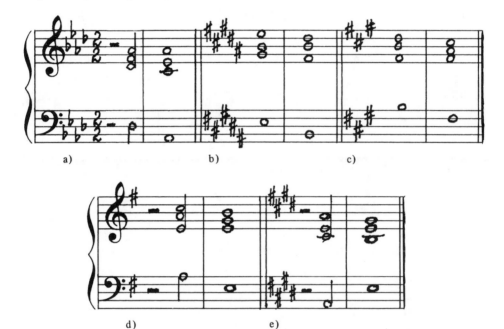

a) b) c)

d) e)

C EXERCISES (p. 80)

1. For each of the following, name the key, write the Roman numeral for each chord, and name the cadence.

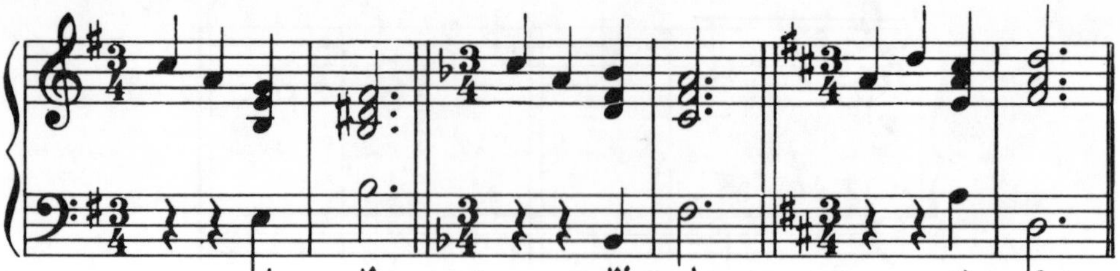

E– Imperfect (I V) — F+ Plagal (IV I) — D+ Perfect (V I)

C– Plagal (IV I) — G– Imperfect (IV V) — A+ Plagal (IV I)

E+ Perfect (V I) — A– Perfect (V I) — B♭+ Plagal (IV I)

2. Write in 2/2 time two different examples of imperfect cadences in each of these keys.

a) D major

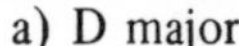

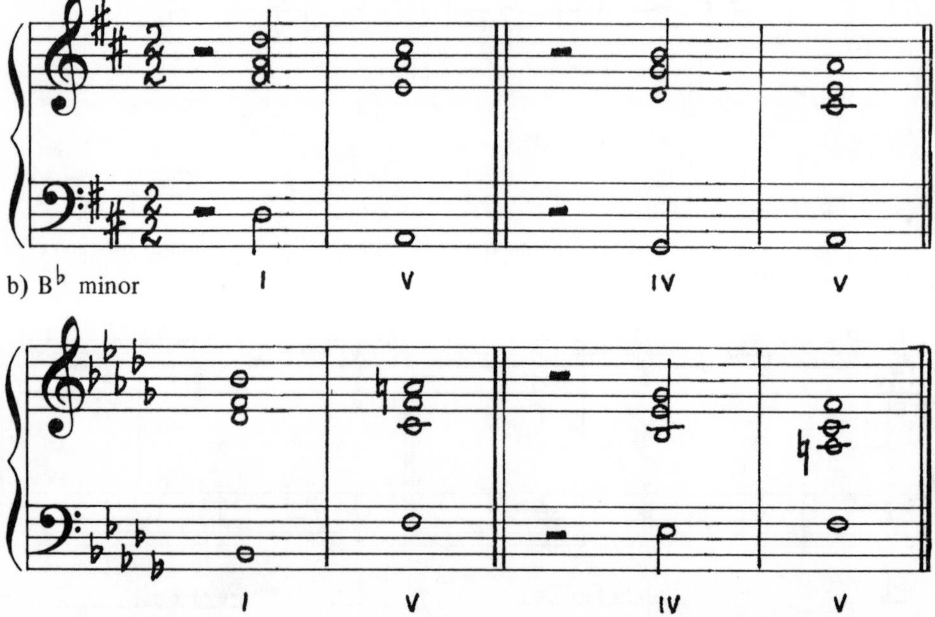

c) G♯ minor
I V IV V
d) A♭ major
I V IV V
e) C minor
I V IV V
e) C♯ minor
I V IV V
f) B major
I V IV V

3. Write in 3/2 time, a two-bar example of each of the three kinds of cadences in each of these keys.

A major

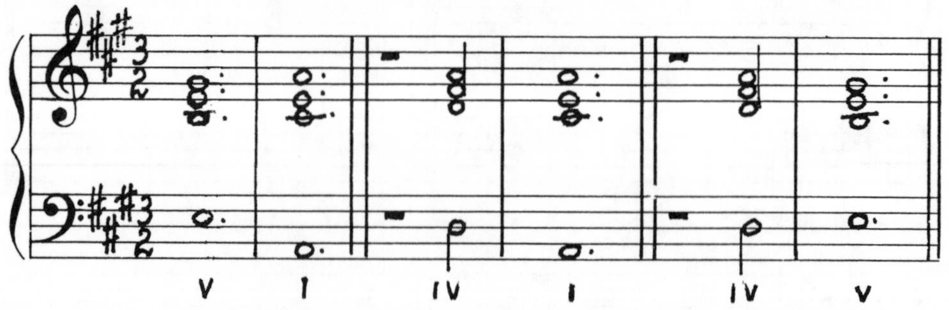

G minor

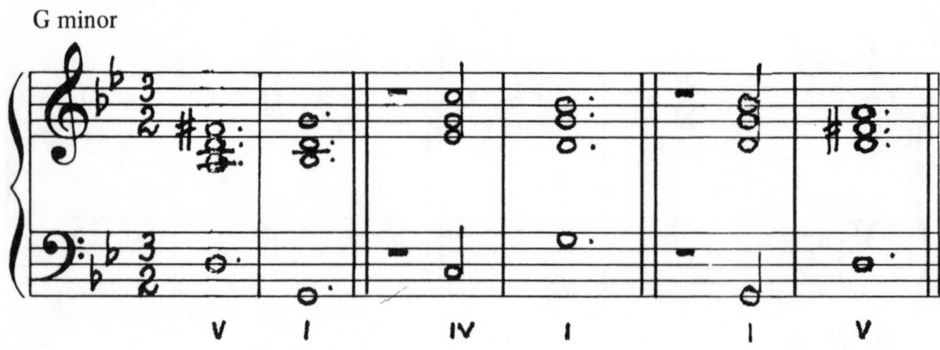

E minor

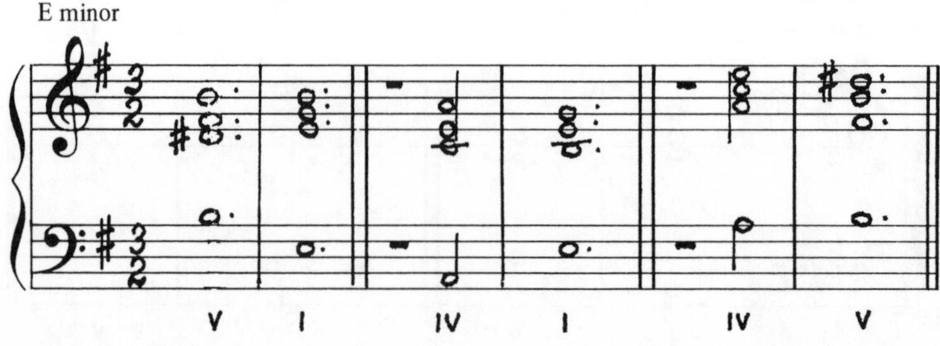

4. Write a cadence at the end of each phrase of the following melodies, and name each cadence.

Perfect
d)
Imperfect
Perfect
e)
Imperfect
Perfect

5. Write a cadence at the end of each phrase of the following melodies, and name each cadence.

e)
Imperfect
Plagal
f)
Imperfect
Perfect
g)
Imperfect
Plagal

h)
Imperfect
Perfect
i)
Imperfect
Plagal
j)
Imperfect
Perfect

C EXERCISES (p. 89)

1. Write the Dominant seventh chord and its inversions in each of the following keys using the correct key signature for each. a) A major b) E♭ major c) B minor d) F minor e) C♯ minor f) B♭ major g) G♯ minor h) D major i) E minor.

2. Solve these Dominant seventh chords.

3. Write these Dominant sevenths in the treble clef, using the correct key signature for each.

a) the first inversion of the Dominant seventh of D minor
b) the second inversion of the Dominant seventh of F♯ minor
c) the root position of the Dominant seventh of B major
d) the third inversion of the Dominant seventh of G minor
e) the root position of the Dominant seventh of E♭ major
f) the first inversion of the Dominant seventh of C♯ minor
g) the second inversion of the Dominant seventh of A major
h) the root position of the Dominant seventh of G♭ major
i) the third inversion of the Dominant seventh of G♯ minor
j) the second inversion of the Dominant seventh of D♭ major

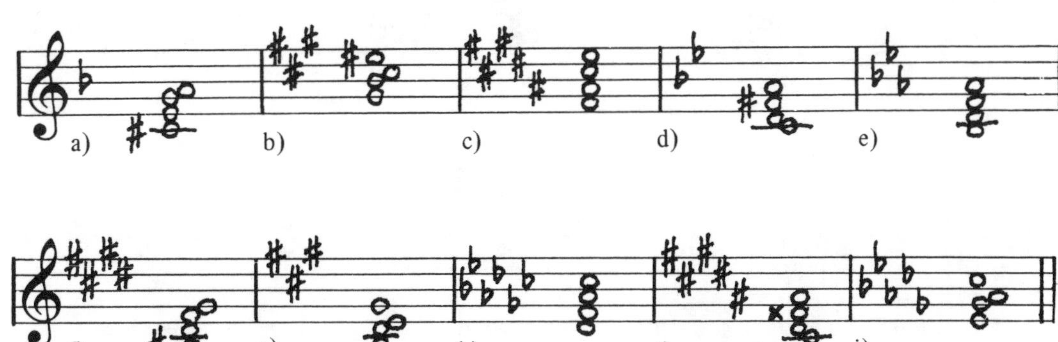

4. Write the Dominant seventh, and inversions of other Dominant sevenths, using F as the lowest note in each case. Name the major key of each.

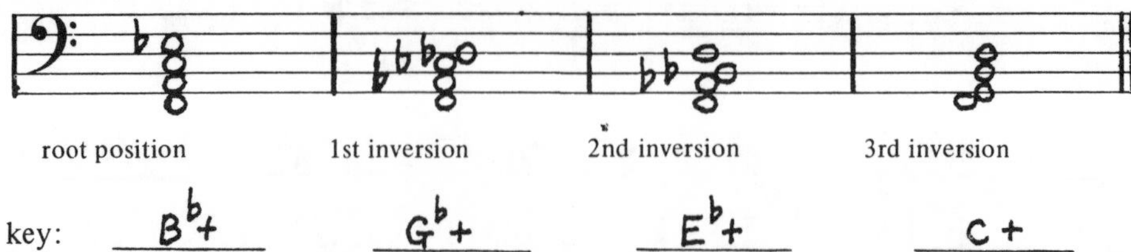

5. Add accidentals to the following to make them into Dominant Seventh chords. Name the minor key of each. **Remember alternative accidentals are possible.**

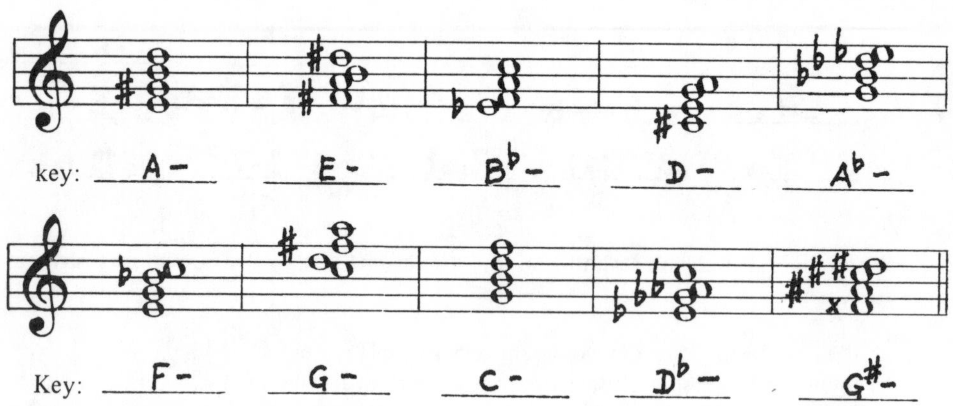

6. Solve these Dominant seventh chords.

root:	F	A	B	E♭	C
key:	B♭+	D+	E−	A♭+	F−
position:	2nd Inv.	2nd Inv.	1st Inv.	2nd Inv.	Root

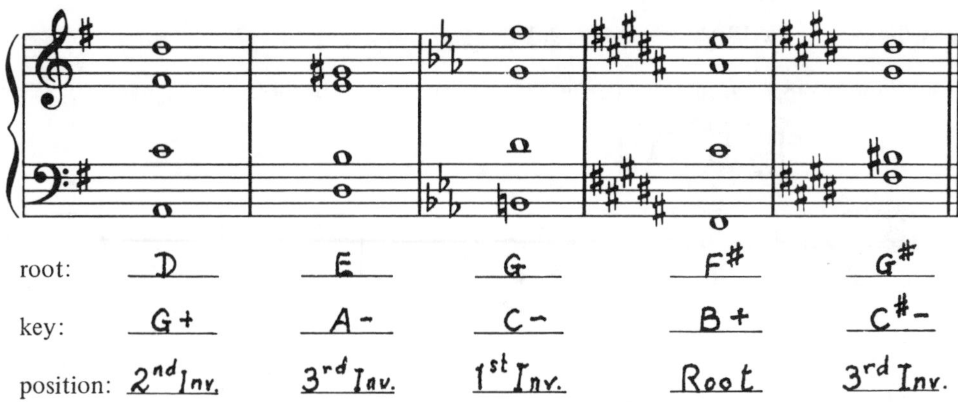

7. Write the Dominant seventh and inversions of other Dominant sevenths, using E as the lowest note for each. Name two keys for each.

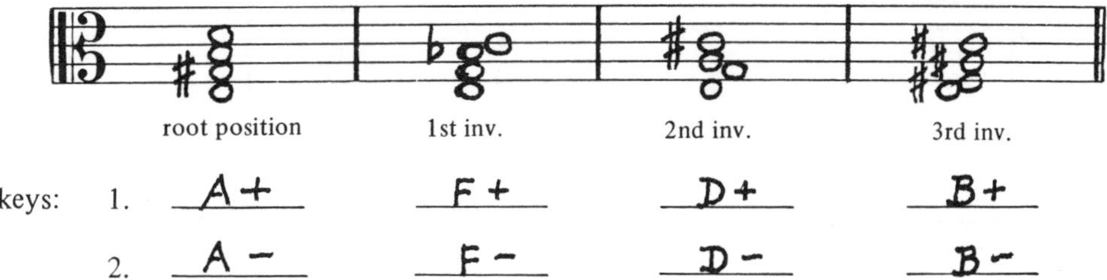

8. Write the Dominant seventh and inversions of other Dominant sevenths using G as the lowest note for each. Name the minor key of each.

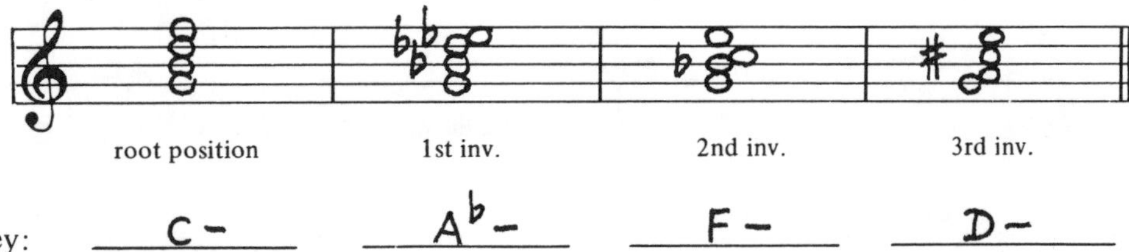

9. Write the Dominant seventh and inversions of other Dominant sevenths using A as the lowest note of each. Name two keys for each.

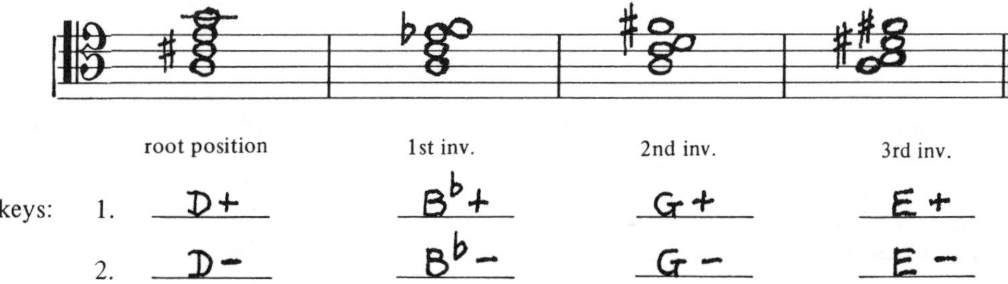

A B C EXERCISES (p. 96)

1. Write two bars, each using a different rhythm, for each of these time signatures. ✱

Example:

a) b)

c) d)

e) f) Breve

g) h)

✱ Obviously many more examples can be given.

2. Add bar lines to each of the following according to the given time signature.

3. Add the correct time signature to each of the following rhythms.

a)

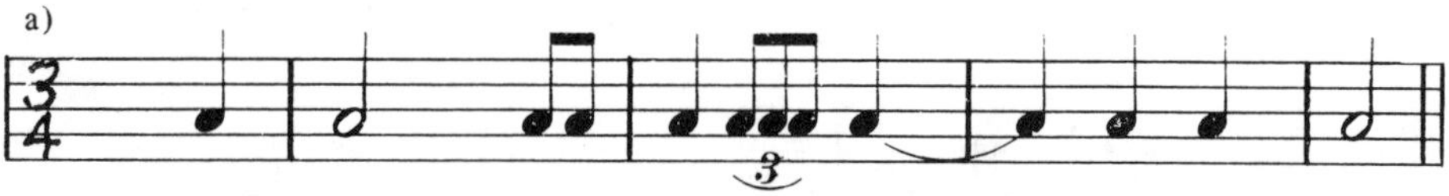

b)

c)

d)

e)

f)

g)

h)

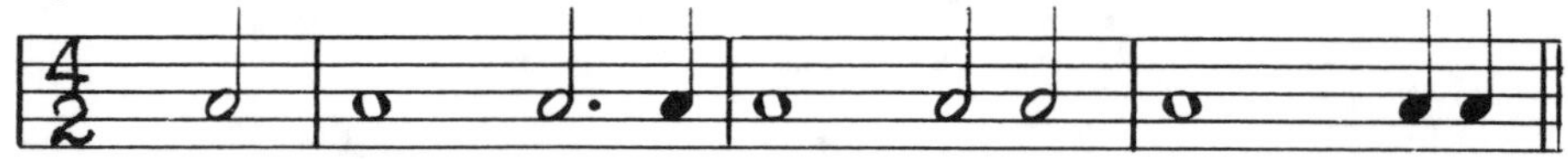

i)

j)

4. Add bar lines to each of the following according to the given time signature.

5. Insert the proper rests in the places indicated by the brackets.

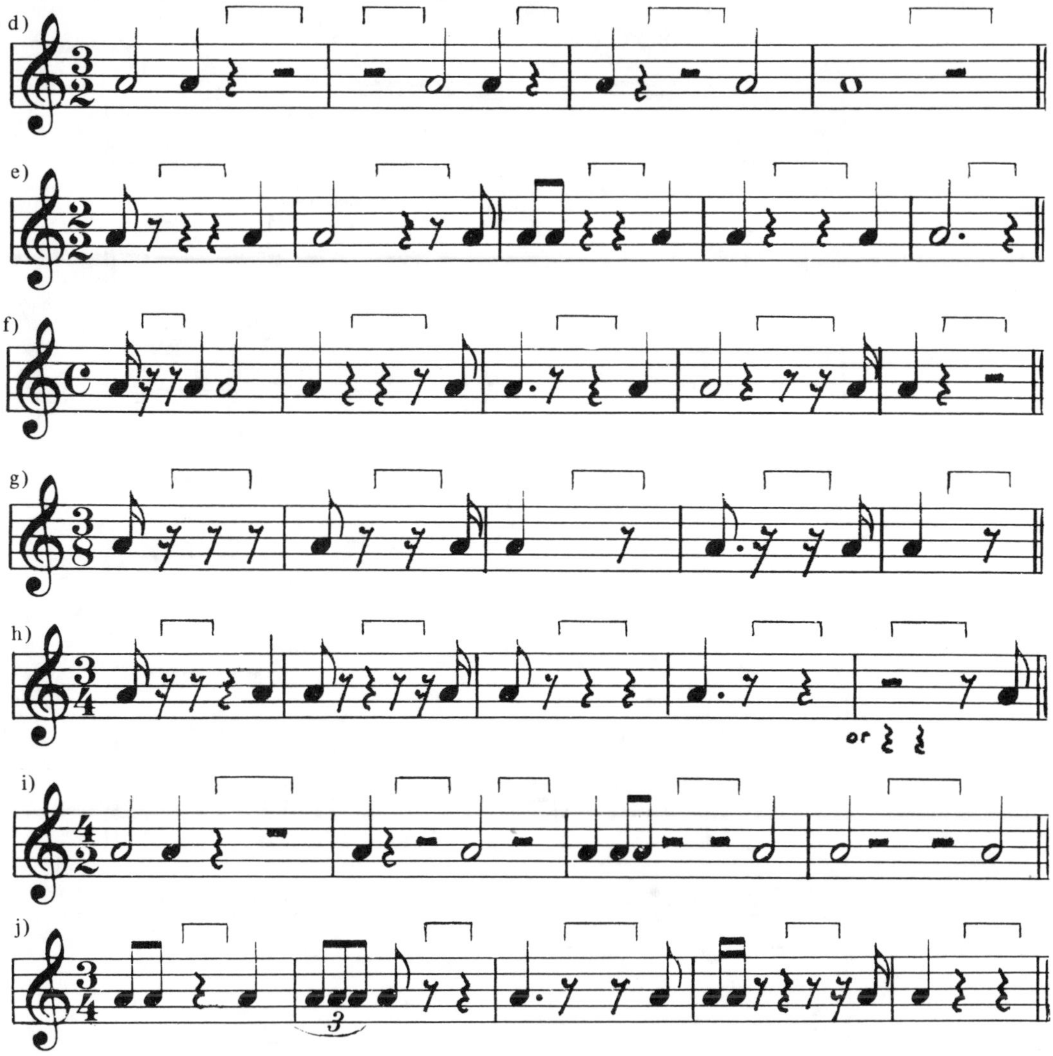

d)

e)

f)

g)

h)

or

i)

j)

6. Add stems to the following and group them correctly to make ONE complete bar of each of these time signatures. *

7. Add the correct time signature to each of the following bars.

a)

b)

c)

d)

e)

f)

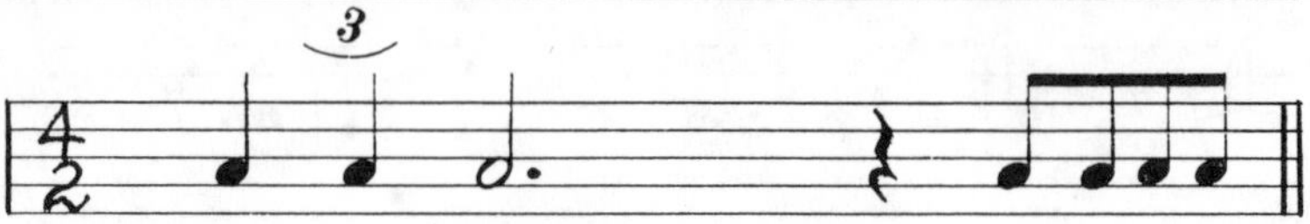

g)

h)

i)

B C EXERCISES (p. 104)

1. Complete the following bars with rests in the places indicated by the brackets.

d)
or
e)
f)
g)
h)
i)
j)

2. Add the correct time signature to each of the following bars:

3. Add stems to the following, and group them correctly, to make ONE complete bar of each of these time signatures. *

* Examples of other groupings are possible.

4. Re-group the following in 6/8 time.

5. Re-group the following in 3/4 time.

6. a) What is the difference between 6/8 time and 3/4 time? b) write one bar of each, grouping the notes correctly.

a) The difference is: – 6/8 time has 2 groups of 3 eighths per bar. and 3/4 time has 3 groups of 2 eighths per bar. – e.g. see top of p. 76.

b)

7. Write three bars, each using a different rhythm, in each of the following time signatures. Dotted notes may be used, but do not use rests. ✱

a)

b)

c)

d)

e)

f)

g)

h)

i)

j)

✱ Many other different arrangements of notes are possible.

8. Complete the following bars with rests.

9. Complete the following bars with rests.

A B C EXERCISES (p. 112)

1. Name the key of this tune. Transpose it down an octave, in the treble clef.

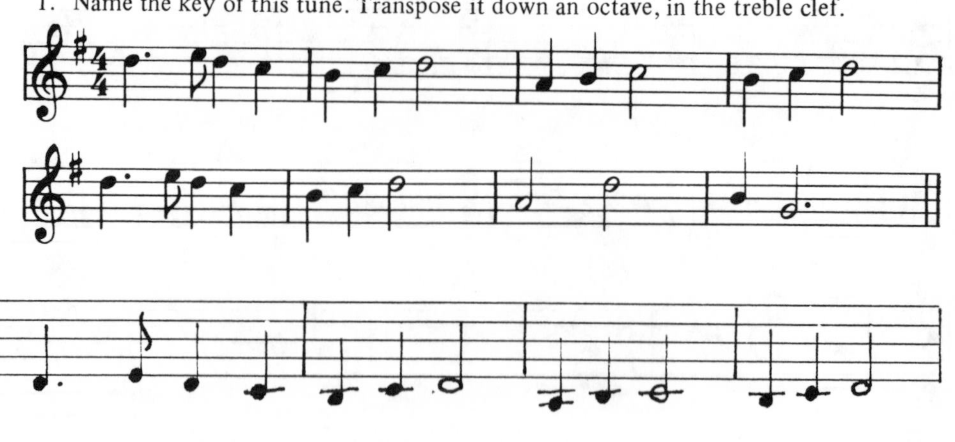

The key is G+

2. Name the key of this tune. Transpose it up an octave, in the bass clef.

The key is E♭+

3. Name the key of this tune. Transpose it up an octave, in the treble clef.

The key is F−

4. Name the key of this tune. Transpose it down an octave in the bass clef.

The key is D+

5. Name the key of this tune. Transpose it down an octave, in the treble clef.

The key is B–

6. Name the key of this tune. Transpose it down an octave in the bass clef.

The key is D–

7. Name the key of this tune. Transpose it up an octave in the treble clef.

The key is A+

8. Name the key of this tune. Transpose it down an octave in the bass clef.

The key is C–

9. Name the key of this tune. Transpose it down an octave in the bass clef.

The key is F+

10. Name the key of this tune. Transpose it up an octave in the treble clef.

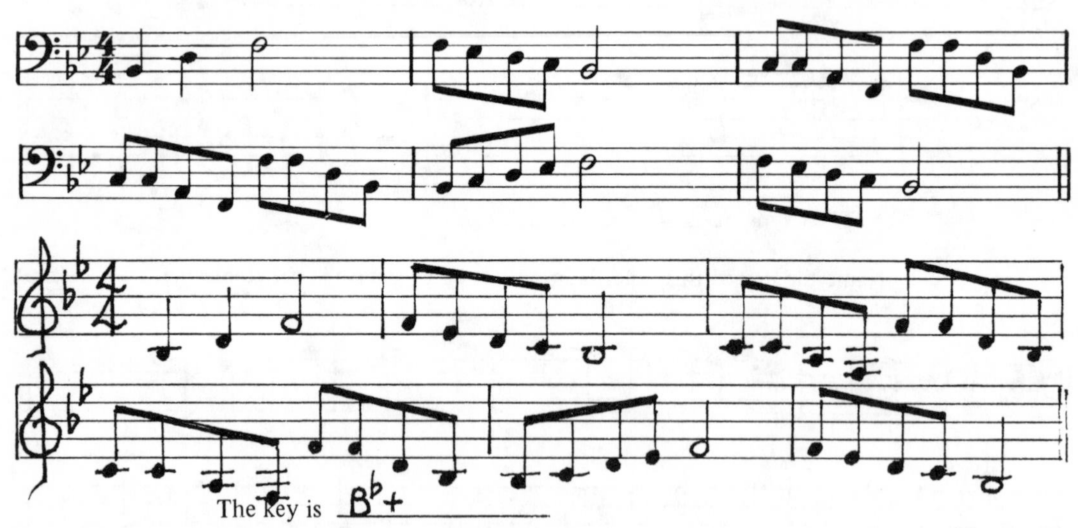

The key is B♭+

11. Name the key of this tune. Transpose it up an octave in the treble clef.

The key is E+

12. Name the key of this tune. Transpose it down an octave in the bass clef.

The key is F♯–

13. Name the key of this tune. Transpose it down an octave in the bass clef.

The key is F–

14. Name the key of this tune. Transpose it down an octave in the treble clef.

The key is B♭+

15. Name the key of this tune. Transpose it down an octave in the bass clef.

The key is D+

B C MORE EXERCISES (p. 116)

1. Name the key of this tune. Re-write it at the same pitch using the correct key signature and omitting any unnecessary accidentals.

The key is G♭+

2. Name the key of this tune. Transpose it down an octave in the bass clef.

The key is E♭+

3. Name the key of this tune. Transpose it down an octave in the bass clef.

The key is G+

4. Re-write this tune at the same pitch in the treble clef, using the correct key signature and omitting any unnecessary accidentals. Name the key.

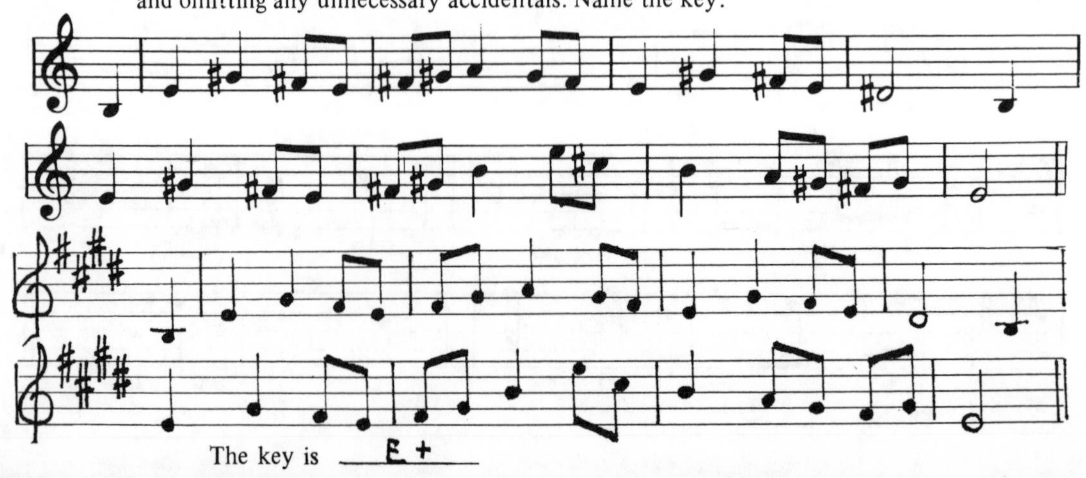

The key is E+

5. Transpose this tune down an octave in the bass clef, using the correct key signature and omitting any unnecessary accidentals. Name the key.

The key is F+

6. Transpose this tune up an octave in the bass clef, using the correct key signature and omitting any unnecessary accidentals. Name the key.

The key is B+

7. Transpose this tune down an octave in the bass clef, using the correct key signature and omitting any unnecessary accidentals. Name the key.

The key is B♭+

8. Transpose this tune up an octave in the bass clef, using the correct key signature and omitting any unnecessary accidentals. Name the key.

The key is A+

C STILL MORE EXERCISES (p. 118)

1. Re-write this tune at the same pitch in the alto clef, using the correct key signature and omitting any unnecessary accidentals. Name the key.

The key is E+

2. Transpose this tune up an octave in the treble clef. Name the key.

The key is D+

3. Re-write this tune at the same pitch in the alto clef, using the correct key signature and omitting any unnecessary accidentals. Name the key.

The key is C–

4. Re-write this tune an octave lower in the alto clef, using the correct key signature and omitting any unnecessary accidentals. Name the key.

The key is B+

B C EXERCISES (p. 121)

1. Transpose the following into A major.

2. Transpose the following a) into F major, b) up a major third.

3. Transpose the following a) into G major b) up a perfect fourth.
a)
b)
4. Transpose the following a) up a major second b) into A major.
a)
b)
5. Transpose the following a) up a perfect fourth, b) up a major second.
a)
b)
6. Transpose the following a) up a major third b) into G major.
a)
b)

7. Transpose the following a) up into the key of B♭ major, b) into F major.

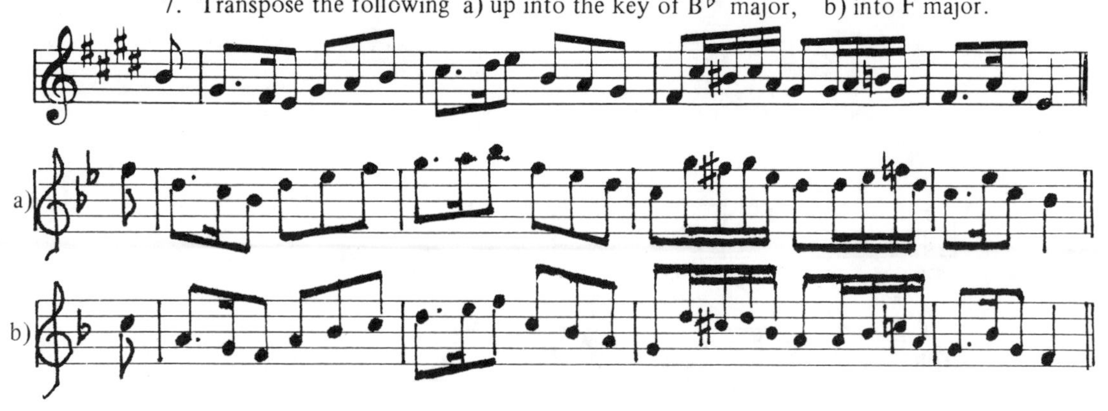

8. In what key is the following tune written? Transpose it into D major, using the correct key signature.

The key is B♭+

9. Transpose the following passage a) into A major, b) up a major third.

10. Transpose the following passage a) into D♭ major, b) up a minor third.

C MORE EXERCISES (p. 124)

1. Transpose the following into D minor.

2. Transpose the following into B minor.

3. Transpose the following into C minor.

4. Transpose the following into F minor.

5. Transpose the following up a minor third in the alto clef.

6. In what key is the following melody written? Transpose it into G minor, using the correct key signature and omitting any unnecessary accidentals.

The key is F♯–

7. In what key is the following melody written? Transpose it down a major third, using the correct key signature and omitting any unnecessary accidentals.

The key is G–

8. In what key is the following passage written? Transpose it a) into G minor and b) into B♭ minor, using the correct key signature, and omitting any unnecessary accidentals.

The key is F–

9. In what key is the following passage written? Transpose it into E minor, using the correct key signature and omitting any unnecessary accidentals.

10. Transpose this passage a) into B minor b) up a major third.

11. In what key is this passage written? Transpose it a) down a minor third, b) up a minor second, using the key signature of the new key and omitting any unnecessary accidentals.

12. Transpose this passage a) into E♭ major b) into B♭ major.

13. Transpose the following passage a) up a minor third b) into B♭ major.

a)

b)

14. Transpose this passage a) into F minor b) into E♭ minor.

a)

b)

C EXERCISES (p. 131)

1. Write the following in short (condensed) score.

2. Write the following passage in open score for string quartet.

3. Write the following passage in modern vocal score.

4. Transpose the above passage into the key of E minor.

5. Write the following passage in open score, using the C clefs for alto and tenor.

6. Transpose the above passage up a major third.

7. Write the following passage in short (condensed) score.

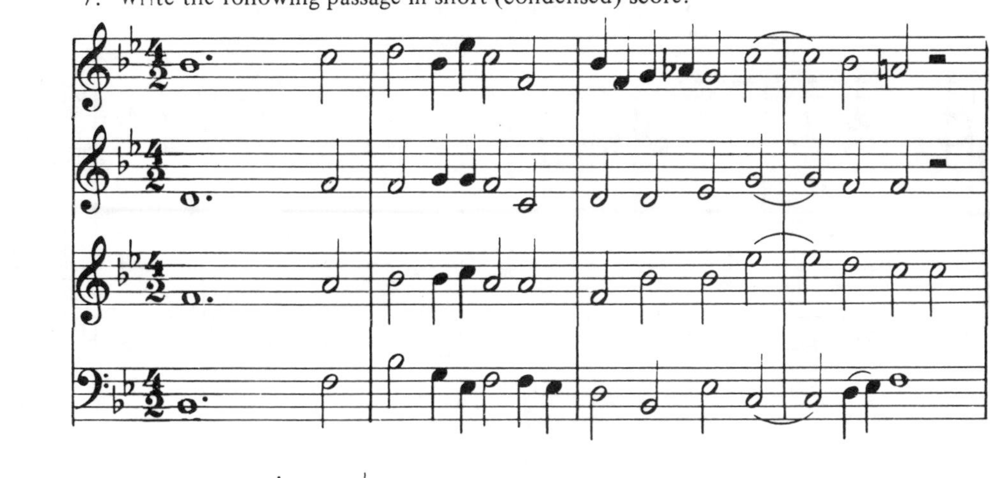

8. Write the following in modern vocal score.

9. Transpose the above passage into A minor.

10. Write the following passage in open score for string quartet.

Moderato

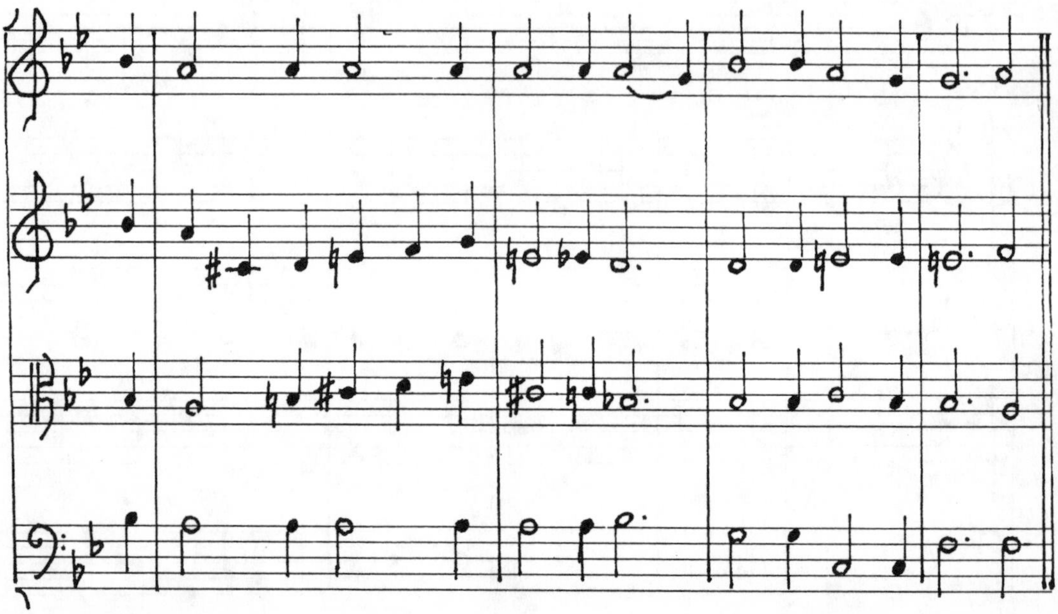

11. Transpose the following passage down a minor third writing it in open score, using the C clefs for alto and tenor.

EXERCISES (p. 137)

B C Re-write the following passages of music, correcting the mistakes.

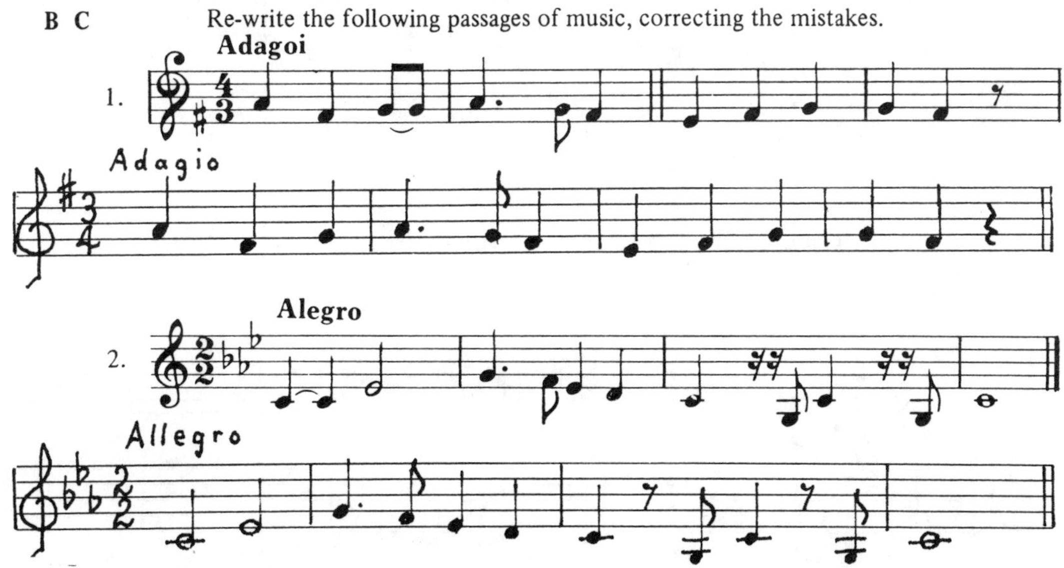

Alle Gretto

3.

Allegretto

moto con

4.

Con moto

dolc

5.

Dolce

Linto

6.

Lento

C MORE EXERCISES (p. 138)

Re-write the following passages of music, correcting the mistakes.

Large
8.
Largo
anima con
9.
Con anima
Poca agitato
10.
Poco agitato
Vivice
11.
Vivace
pui tranquillo
12.
Piu tranquillo

A **TEST PAPER # 1** (p. 169)

Marks allotted

6 I Name these notes.

6 II Name these notes.

6 III Beside each of these notes, write the note which is a chromatic semitone below.

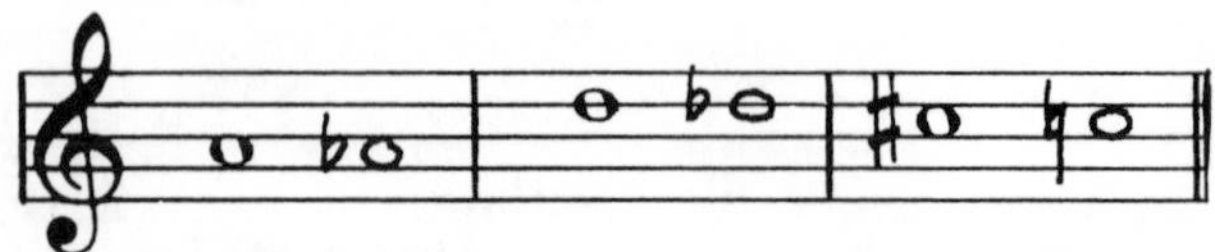

6 IV Beside each of these notes, write the note which is a diatonic semitone below.

10 V Write in the bass clef the scales of A major and C minor harmonic ascending and descending, using the correct key signature for each. Mark the semitones with a slur.

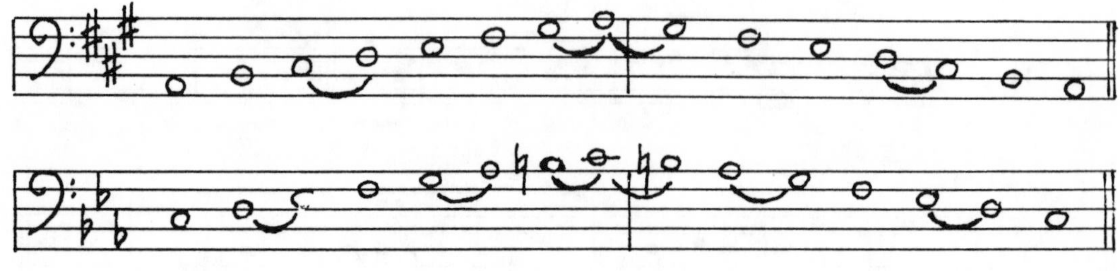

10 VI Write in the treble clef the scales of D minor melodic and E♭ major, ascending and descending, using accidentals instead of a key signature. Mark the semitones with a slur.

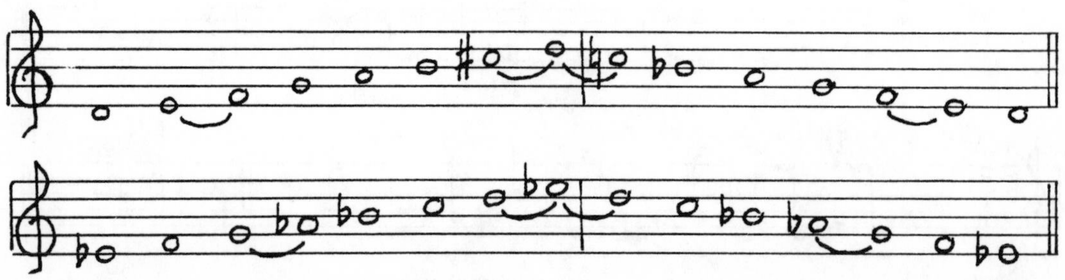

6 VII Write the dominant triads of F major, B♭ major and E minor in the treble clef.

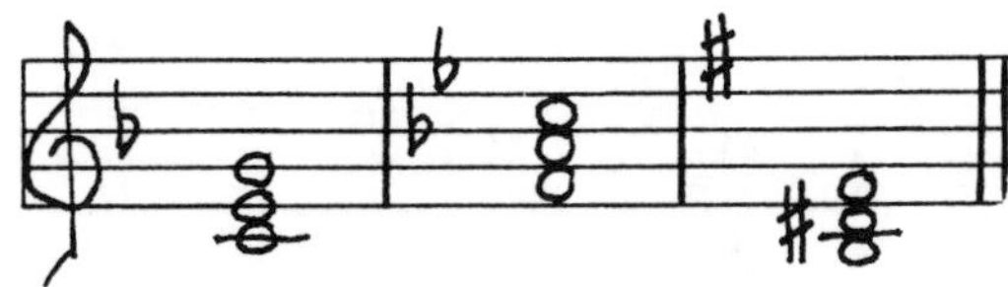

6 VIII Write the tonic triads of D major, A minor and A♭ major in the bass clef.

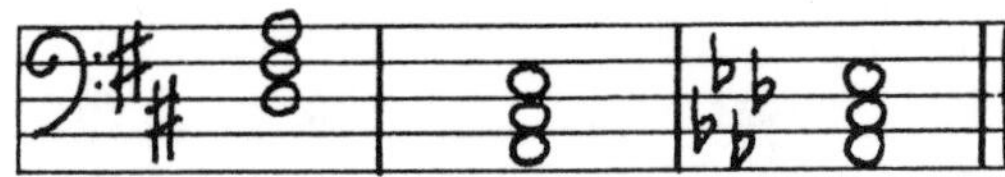

10 IX Transpose this melody one octave higher in the treble clef. Name the key.

Key: F +

10 X Complete the following bars with rests.

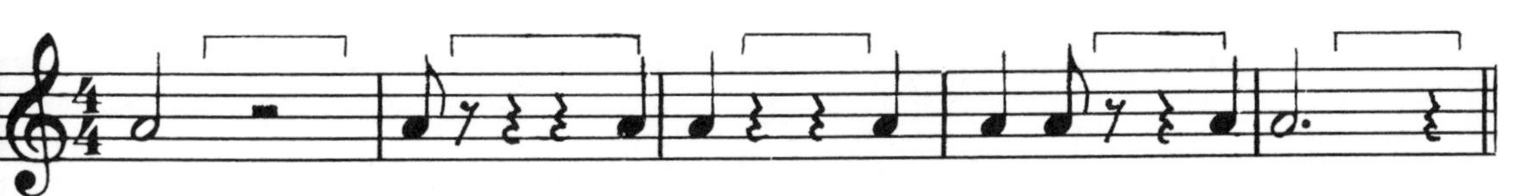

10 XI Explain the following signs:

a) 𝄐 Pause. Hold the note or rest longer than its value.

b) ─< Crescendo. Get gradually louder.

c) *ff* Fortissimo. Very loud.

d) :|| Repeat. Play the previous section again.

e) ♮ Natural. Play the note at its original pitch.

14 XII Name the following intervals.

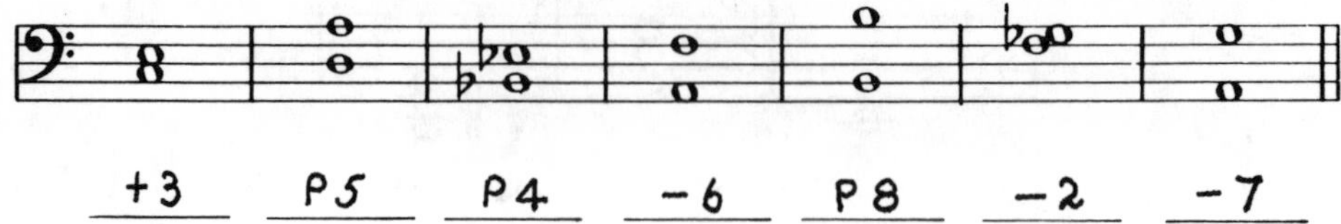

A

TEST PAPER # 2 (p. 172)

Marks allotted

10 I Write the following as half notes in the bass clef.

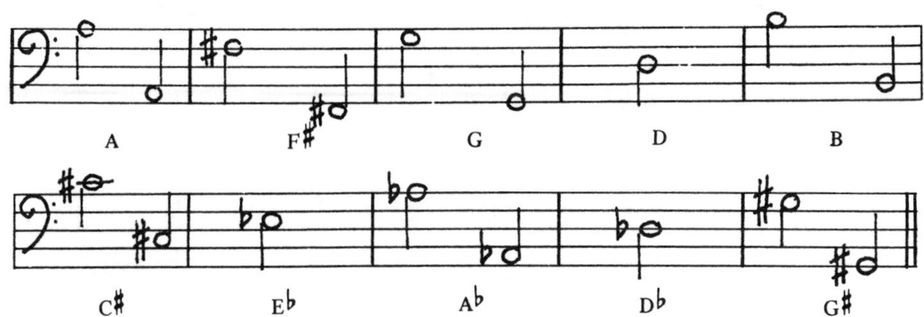

8 II Beside each of these notes, write the note that is a tone above.

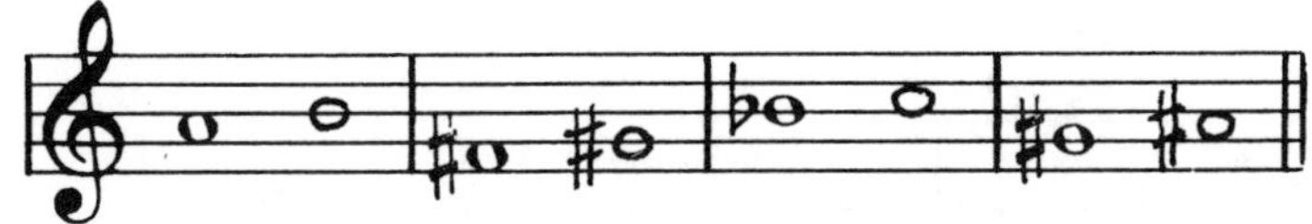

6 III Beside each of these notes, write the note that is a chromatic semitone above.

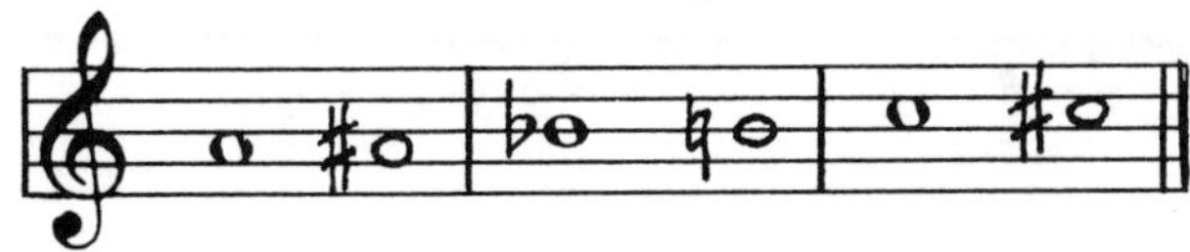

10 IV Write the following scales in the treble clef, ascending and descending, using the correct key signature for each. Mark the semitones with a slur.

a) D major in quarter notes

b) E minor melodic in whole notes

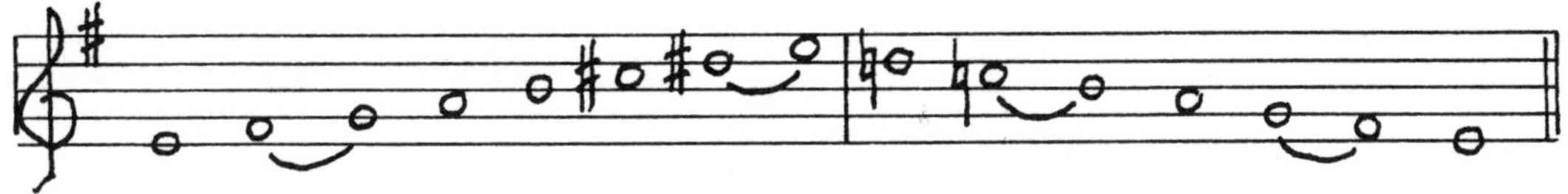

c) G minor harmonic in half notes

d) A♭ major in eighth notes

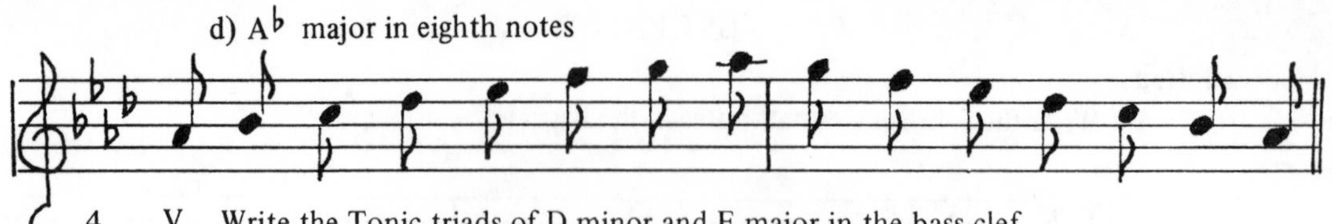

4 V Write the Tonic triads of D minor and E major in the bass clef.

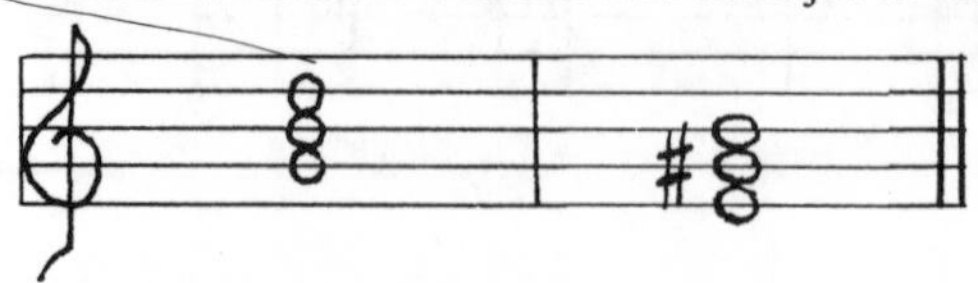

4 VI Write the Dominant triads of C minor and A major in the treble clef.

6 VII Name the key of each of the following melodies

8 VIII Explain the following terms:

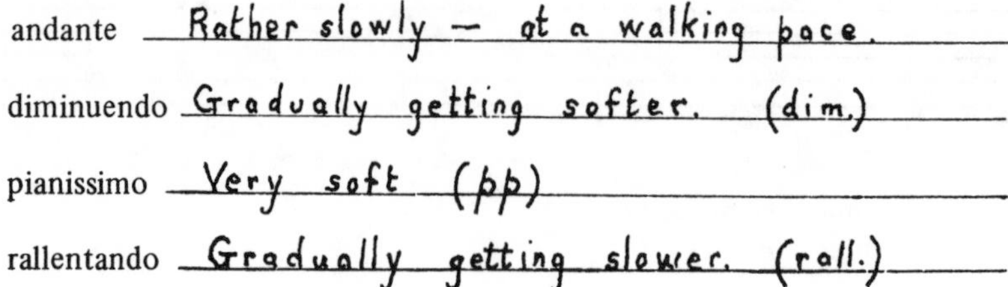

andante Rather slowly – at a walking pace.

diminuendo Gradually getting softer. (dim.)

pianissimo Very soft (pp)

rallentando Gradually getting slower. (rall.)

12 IX Add the correct time signature to the beginning of each of these bars.

6 X Transpose this melody one octave lower in the bass clef. Name the key.

6 XI Transpose this melody one octave higher in the treble clef. Name the key.

14 XII Name these intervals.

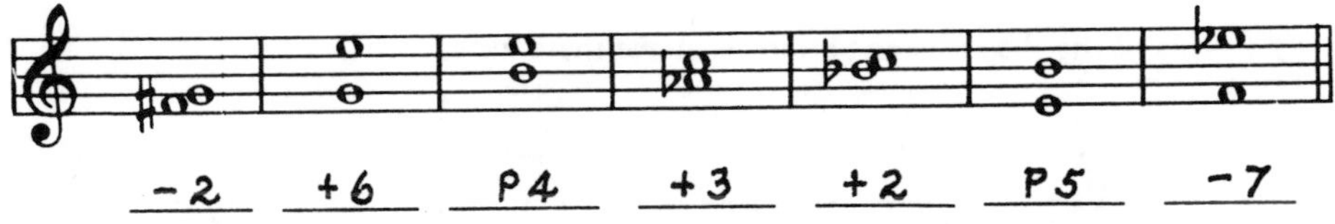

Marks allotted A

TEST PAPER # 3 (p. 175)

10 I Write the following scales ascending and descending.

a) A major in half notes in the treble clef, using the correct key signature. Mark the semitones with a slur.

b) F minor melodic in quarter notes in the bass clef, using the correct key signature. Mark the semitones with a slur.

10 II Complete the following bars with rests.

10 III Write the following intervals above these notes

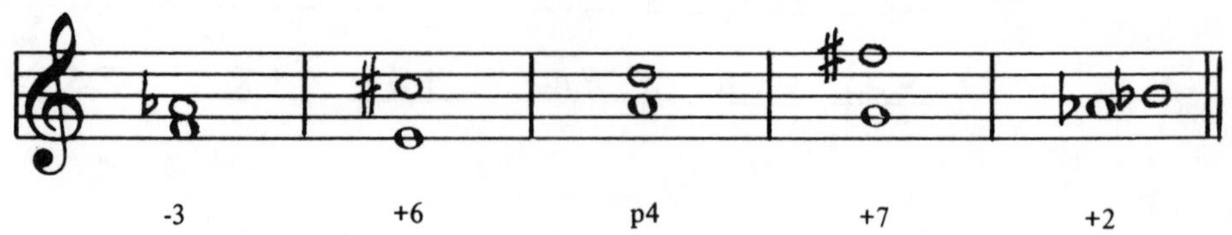

6 IV Explain the following:

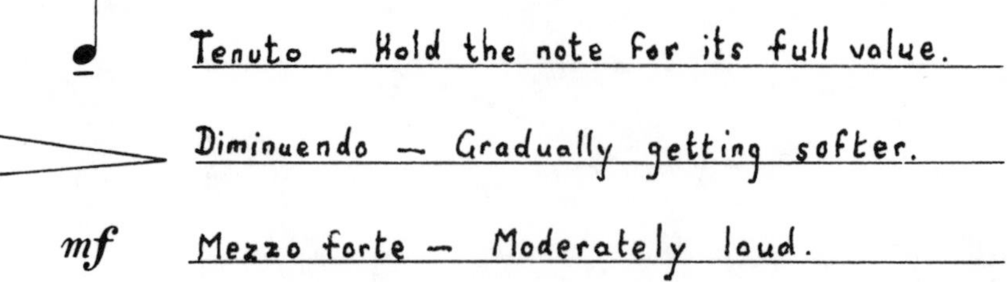

10 V Beside each of the following notes write the note that is a diatonic semitone above.

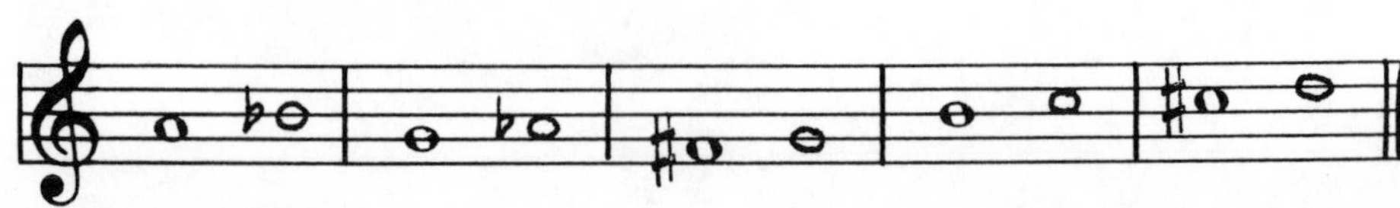

10 VI Write the following notes as half notes in the bass clef.

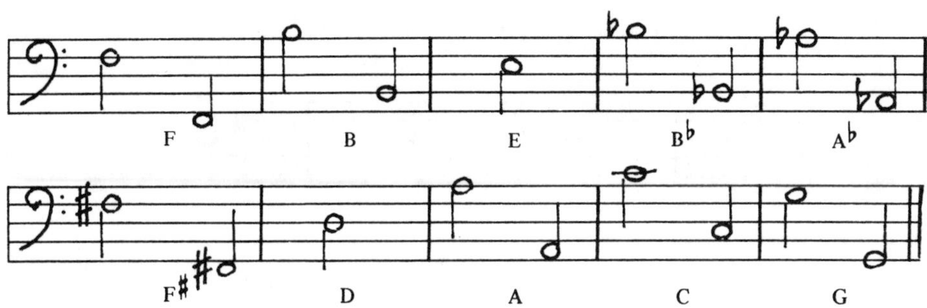

10 VII Transpose this melody one octave lower in the bass clef. Name the key.

10 VIII Beside each of the following notes, write the note that is a whole tone above.

8 IX Add the correct time signature to each of these bars.

8 X Write in the treble clef the following key-signatures

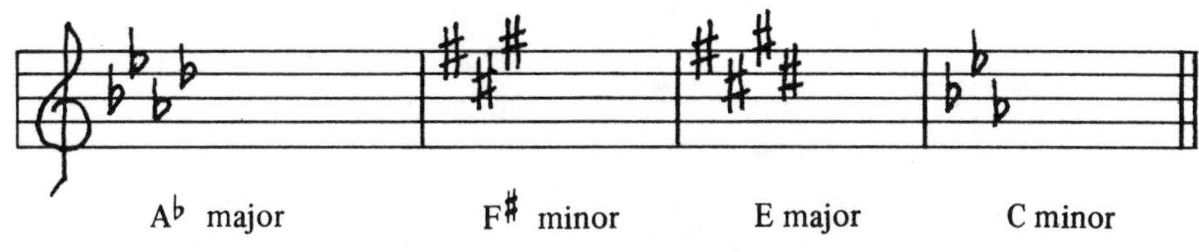

8 XI Write in the bass clef, the Tonic and Dominant triads of each of these keys: F minor; D major.

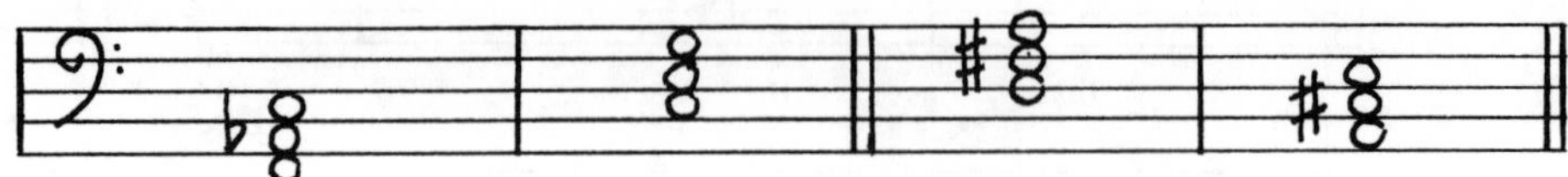

TEST PAPER # 4 (p. 178)

B

Marks allotted

8 I Write the following notes in the bass clef, using the correct key signature for each.

a) the Dominant of B major
b) the Mediant of D♭ major
c) the Leading note of C♯ minor
d) the Supertonic of E♭ minor

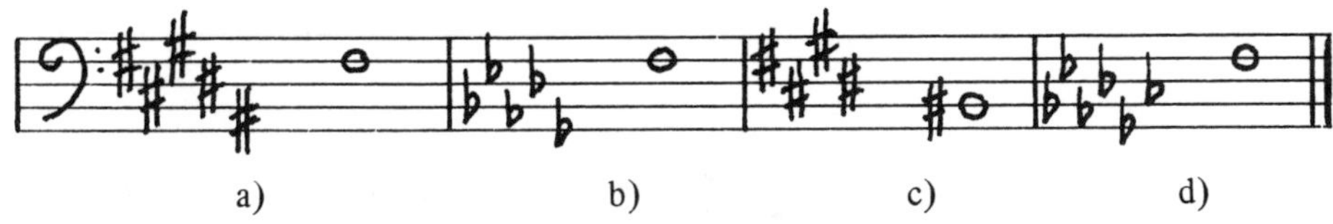

12 II Write the following scales, ascending and descending, in the treble clef, using accidentals instead of key signatures.

a) F minor melodic

b) G♭ major

c) B♭ minor harmonic

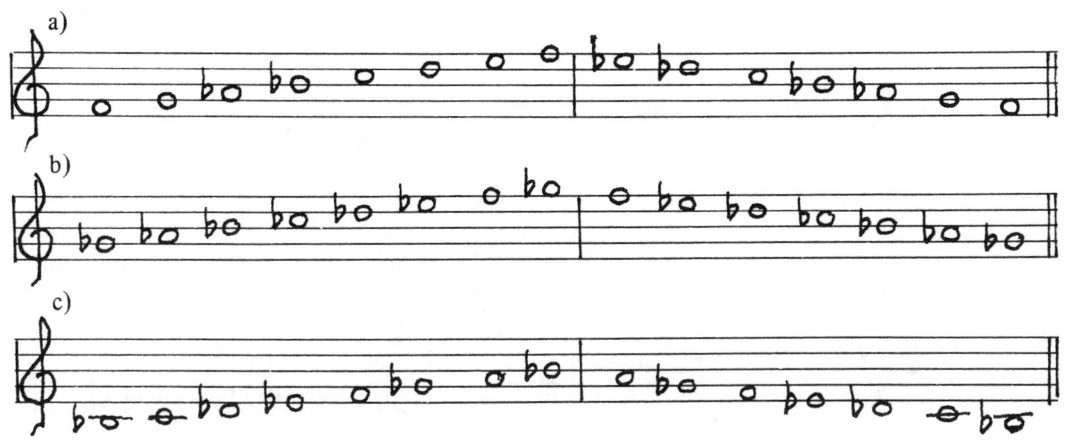

8 III Explain the following Italian terms:

a) cantabile In a singing style

b) dolce Sweetly

c) meno mosso Less movement

d) sforzando Strongly accented

12 IV Write the following triads in the treble clef.

a) the root position of D major

b) the first inversion of E♭ major

c) the root position of B minor

d) the second inversion of A major

e) the first inversion of C minor

f) the root position of B major.

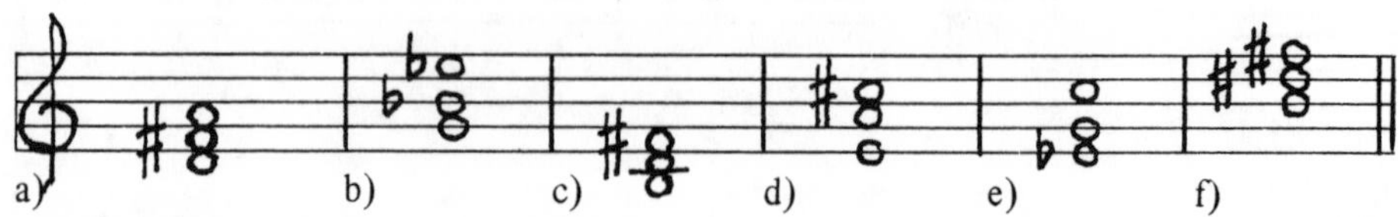

12 V Name the following intervals. Invert them and name what you have written.

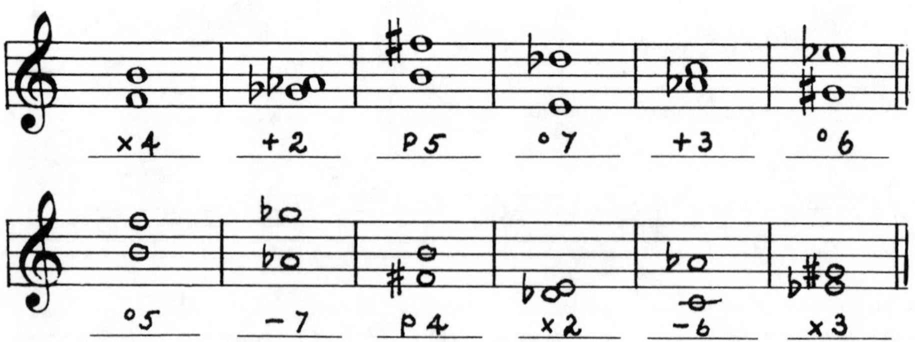

8 VI Copy the following passage at the same pitch; supply the correct key signature; omit the unnecessary accidentals, and name the key.

10 VII Complete the following bars with rests.

10 VIII Re-write the following passage, correcting the mistakes.

12 IX Write in 2/2 time, a two-bar example of each of the following:

a) a plagal cadence in A major

b) a perfect cadence in G minor

c) a perfect cadence in A♭ major

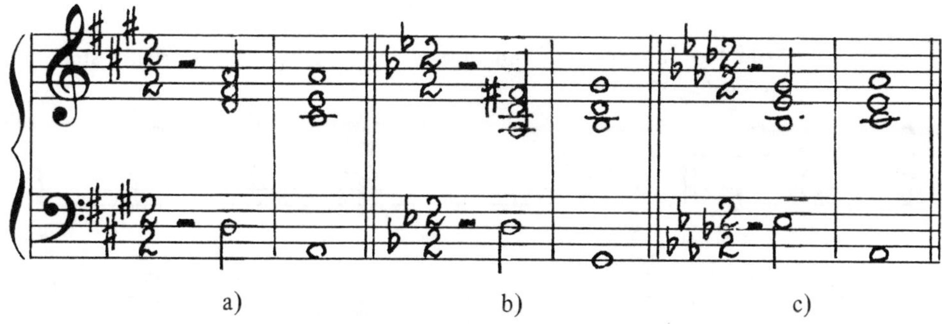

a) b) c)

8 X Transpose the following passage up a major second.

B **TEST PAPER # 5** (p. 181)

Marks allotted

12 I Add the proper clef, key signature, and accidentals where necessary to form the following scales:

12 II Write the root position and inversions of each of these triads. State whether each triad is major or minor.

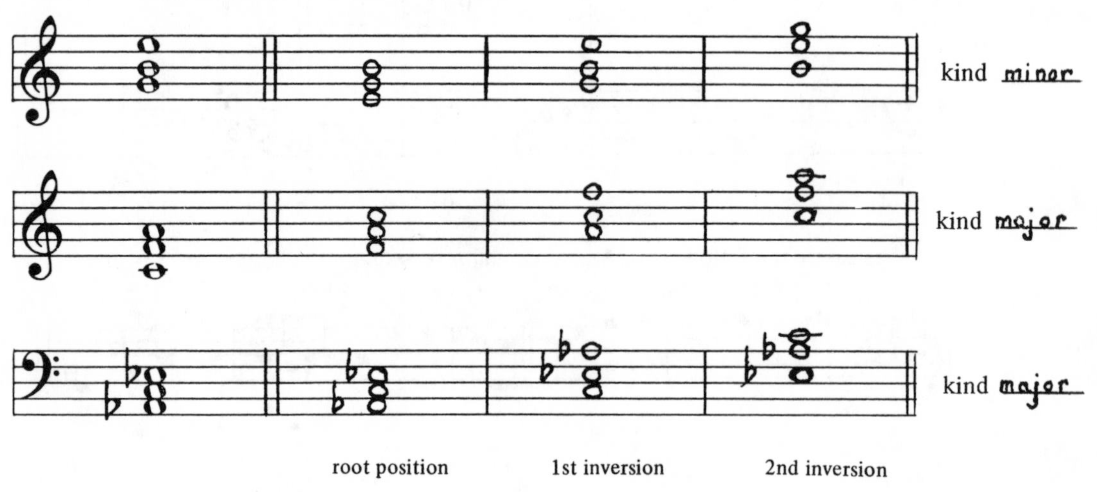

8 III Copy the following passage at the same pitch. Supply the correct key signature, omit unnecessary accidentals and name the key.

8 IV Transpose the following passage into F major.

12 V Write the following intervals above the given notes. Invert them and name what you have written.

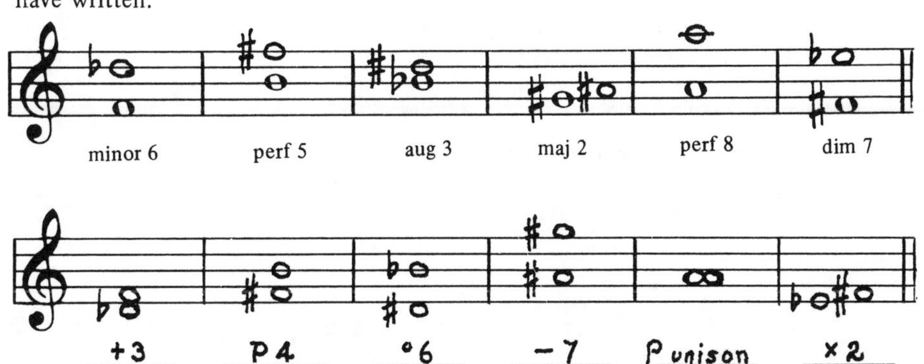

8 VI Give the English meaning for each of these Italian terms.

a) allegretto moderately fast

b) diminuendo gradually softer

c) molto much

d) pesante heavily

12 VII Write in 3/4 time a two-bar example of each of the following cadences:

a) a perfect cadence in F minor

b) a plagal cadence in B major

c) a plagal cadence in C♯ minor

8 VIII Write the following notes in the bass clef, using the correct key signature for each.

a) the leading note of G sharp minor

b) the submediant of A major

c) the supertonic of E♭ minor

d) the dominant of B minor.

10 IX Re-write the following passage, correcting the mistakes.

10 X Complete the following bars with rests.

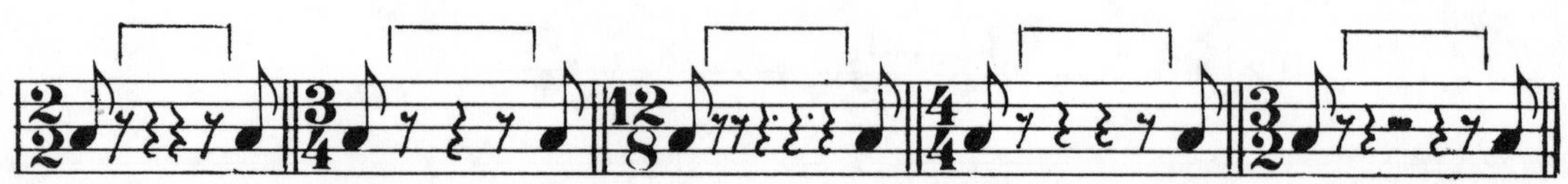

B **TEST PAPER # 6** (p. 184)

Marks allotted

12 I Write the following scales in the bass clef, ascending and descending, using the correct key signature for each.

a) E major
b) its relative minor (melodic form)
c) its tonic minor (harmonic form)

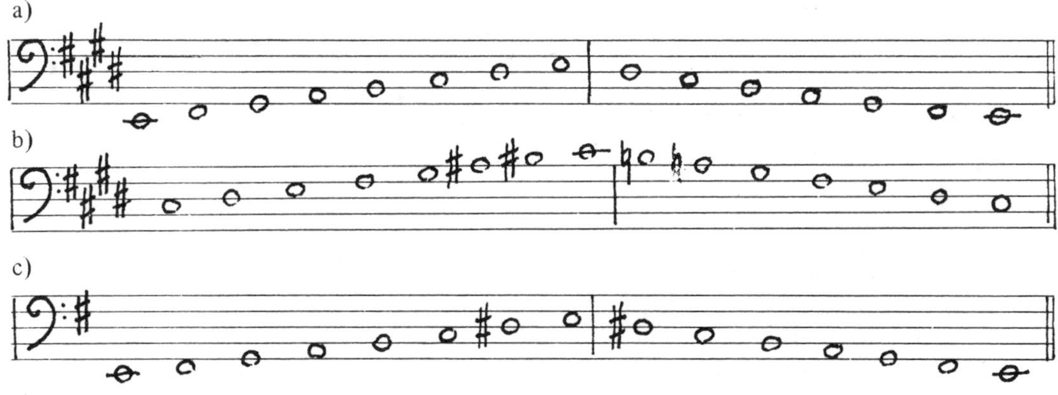

6 II Transpose the following melody up a major third.

15 III Name the following intervals. Invert them and name what you have written.

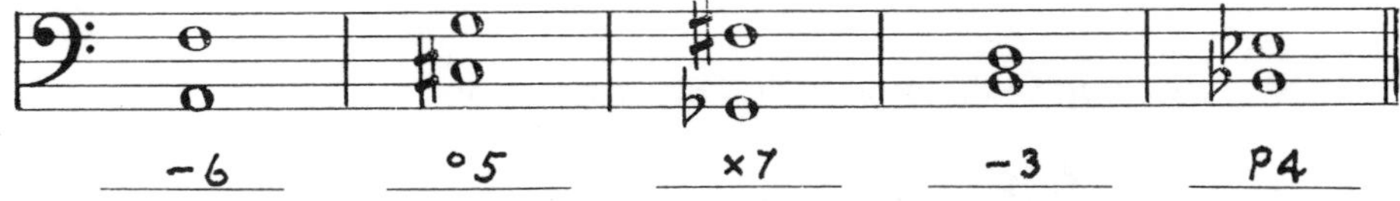

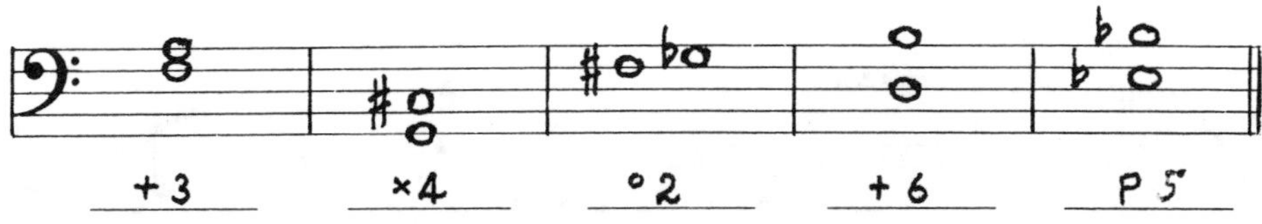

7 IV Fill in the blanks.

The Mediant of E major is G♯

The Dominant of C♯ minor is G♯

The Supertonic of A♭ major is B♭

The Tonic of B major is B

The Leading Note of F minor is E♮

The Submediant of D♭ major is B♭

The Subdominant of G♯ minor is C♯

12 V Write the following triads in the treble clef.

a) a major triad with E as the root

b) a minor triad with F as the third

c) a minor triad with B♭ as the root

d) a major triad with G as the fifth.

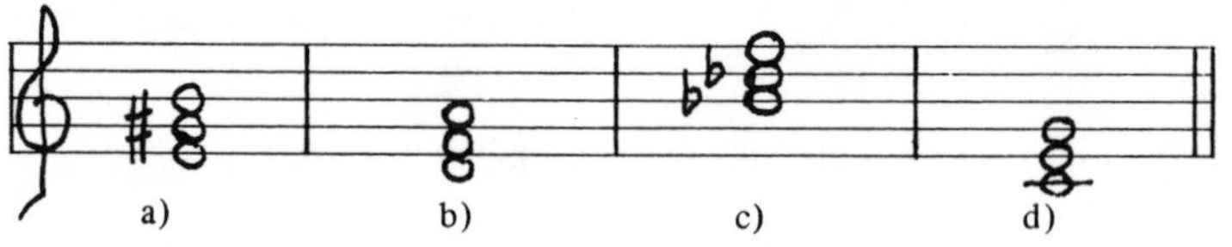

10 VI Complete each of the following bars with rests.

10 VII Correct the errors in the following passage.

8 VIII Give the Italian term usually used to mean the following:

a) gradually getting slower rallentando

b) very softly pianissimo

c) with fire con fuoco

d) playfully scherzando

8 IX Copy this tune at the same pitch. Use the correct key signature. Omit the unnecessary accidentals and name the key.

Key: E♭ +

12 X Write in 2/2 time a two-bar example of each of the following:

a) a plagal cadence in A major

b) a perfect cadence in C minor

c) a perfect cadence in B major

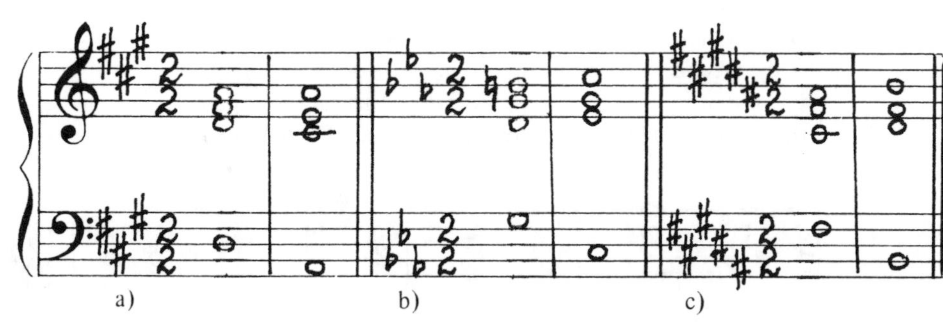

C TEST PAPER # 7 (p. 187)

Marks allotted

16 I Add the correct clef, key signature and accidentals where necessary, to the following notes to form these scales:

a) E flat major from Mediant to Mediant
b) C minor melodic from Subdominant to Subdominant
c) A major from Dominant to Dominant
d) G sharp minor harmonic from Supertonic to Supertonic

a) 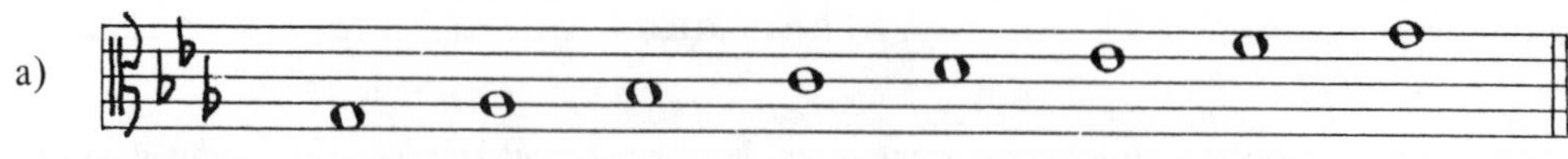

b) 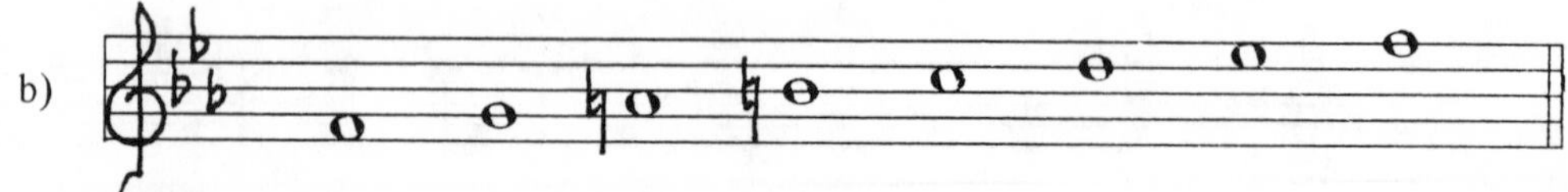

c) 

d) 

12 II Write the following intervals in the alto clef, using E flat as the upper note in each case. a) minor third, b) diminished fourth, c) perfect fifth, d) minor second, and e) minor seventh.

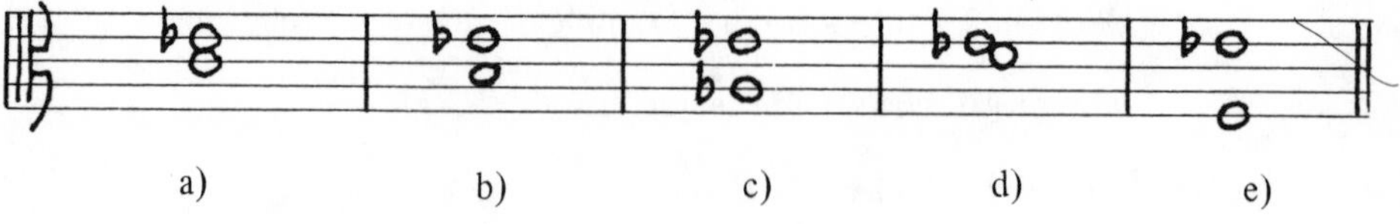

a) b) c) d) e)

What key contains all the above intervals? C–

10 III Write the following triads in the bass clef, using the correct key signature for each.

a) the first inversion of the Subdominant triad of E flat major
b) the root position of the Supertonic triad of F minor
c) the second inversion of the Dominant triad of B minor
d) the root position of the Leading note triad of C sharp major
e) the second inversion of the Mediant triad of G flat major

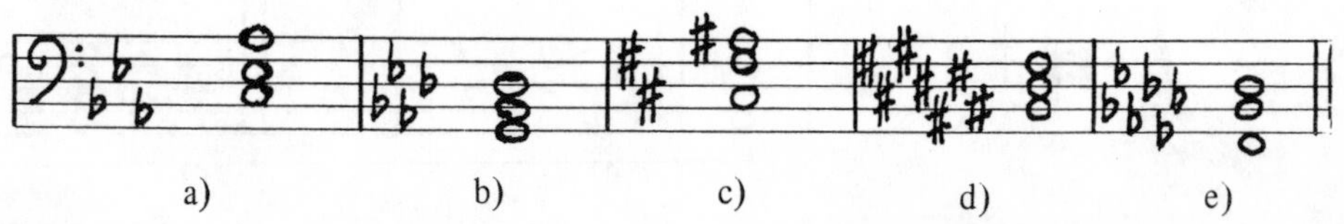

a) b) c) d) e)

8 IV Write in the treble clef a dominant seventh, and inversions of other dominant sevenths, each having E as the lowest note.

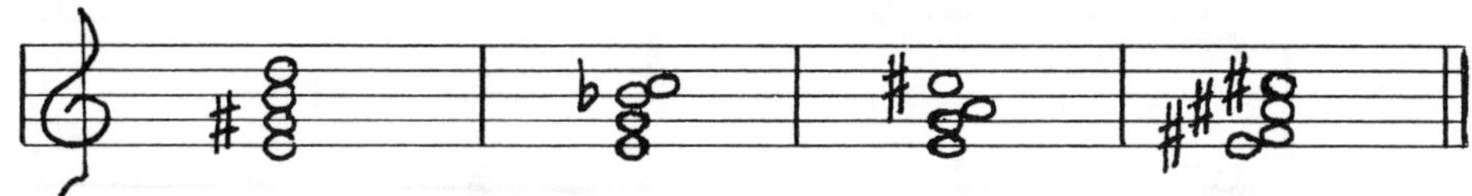

8 V Write a cadence at the end of each phrase of the following melody, and name each cadence.

Imperfect

10 VI Transpose the following melody up a diminished fifth.

10 VII Write the following in modern vocal score.

6 VIII Give the usual English meaning for these Italian terms:

a) a piacere At one's own wish.

b) stringendo Hurrying on the time.

c) strepitoso Noisy, boisterous.

11 IX Re-write the following passage, correcting the errors.

9 X Add stems to the following to make ONE complete bar of each of the following time signatures. Group each correctly. ✱

✱ Examples of other groupings are possible

C TEST PAPER # 8 (p. 191)

Marks allotted

12 I Write the following scales in the alto clef, ascending and descending, using the correct key signature for each.

a) A major, from Mediant to Mediant
b) its relative minor melodic, from Dominant to Dominant
c) its tonic minor harmonic, from Submediant to Submediant
d) a harmonic chromatic scale starting on A

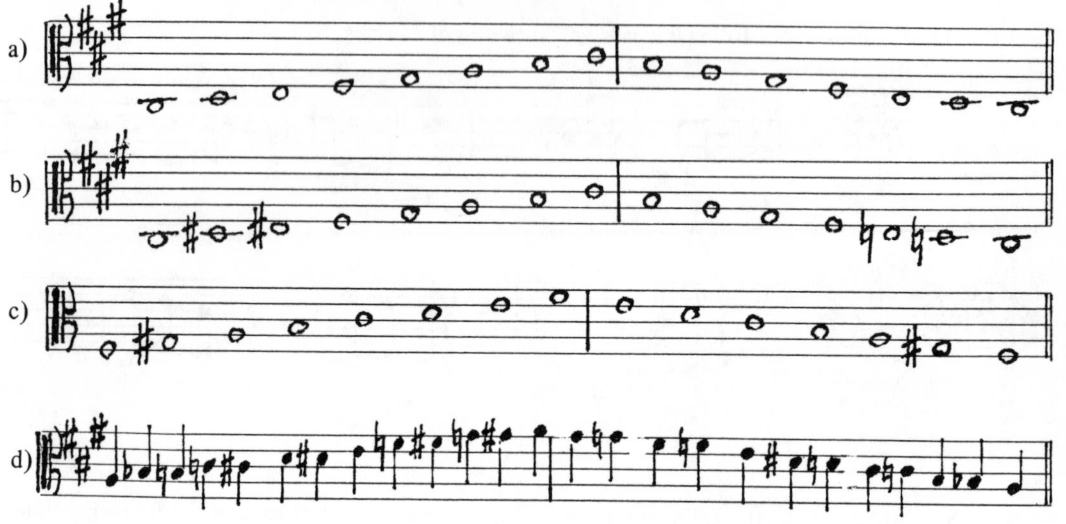

10 II Name this interval. Invert it in the tenor clef and rename.

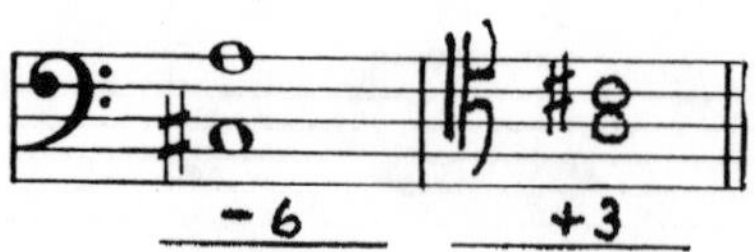

Name all the keys in which these intervals may be found.

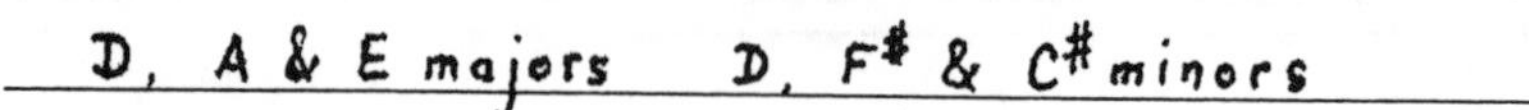

8 III Add the correct time signature to each of the following.

12 IV For each of the following triads give a) the root b) the kind of triad c) the position.

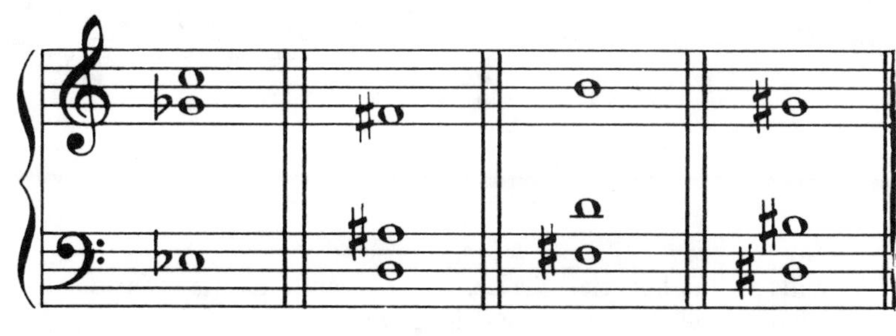

a) root:	C	D	B	G#
b) kind:	Dim.	Aug.	Minor	Major
c) position:	1st inv.	Root	2nd inv.	2nd inv.

8 V Write a cadence at the end of each phrase of the following melody, and name each cadence.

8 VI Complete the following bars with rests.

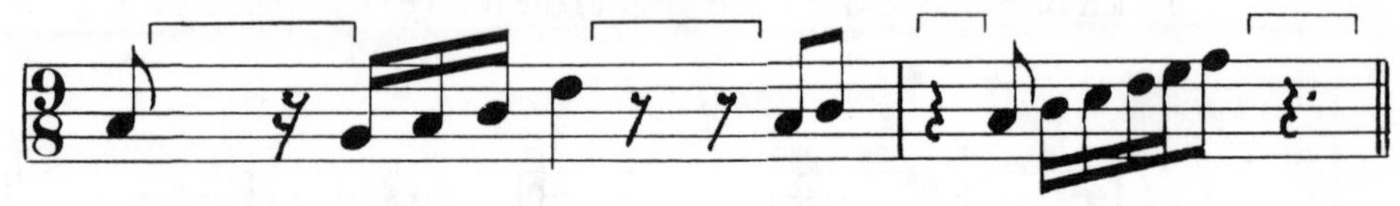

8 VII Write in the bass clef, the dominant seventh and its inversions in the key of F sharp minor, using the correct key signature.

9 VIII Name all the keys in which each of these triads may be found.

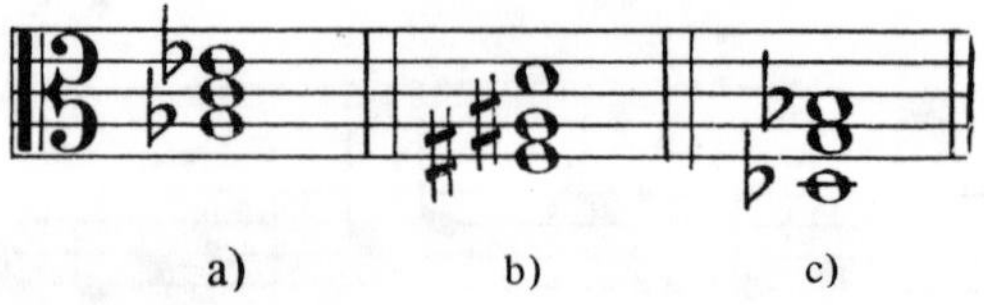

a) A♭+, E♭+, D♭+, (D♭−), C−

b) B−

c) A♭+, A♭−, F−

16 IX Transpose the following passage into B♭ major, writing in open score for string quartet.

9 X Rewrite the following passage, correcting the mistakes.

C **TEST PAPER # 9** (p. 196)

Marks allotted

16 I Write the following scales ascending and descending in the bass clef.

a) A flat major from leading note to leading note

b) F minor melodic from mediant to mediant

c) A flat minor harmonic from supertonic to supertonic

d) G sharp minor harmonic from dominant to dominant

State the relationship of each of the last three scales to the first.

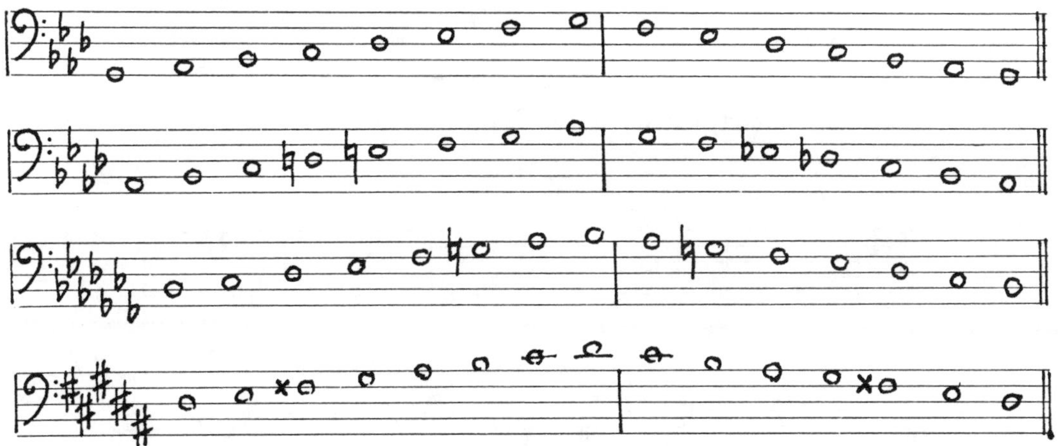

Relationship:– F – is the relative minor of A♭ +

A♭ – is the tonic minor of A♭ +

G♯ – is the enharmonic tonic minor of A♭ +

12 II Write the following in open score, using the C clefs for alto and tenor.

12 III Name the following intervals. Change the upper note of each enharmonically and rename.

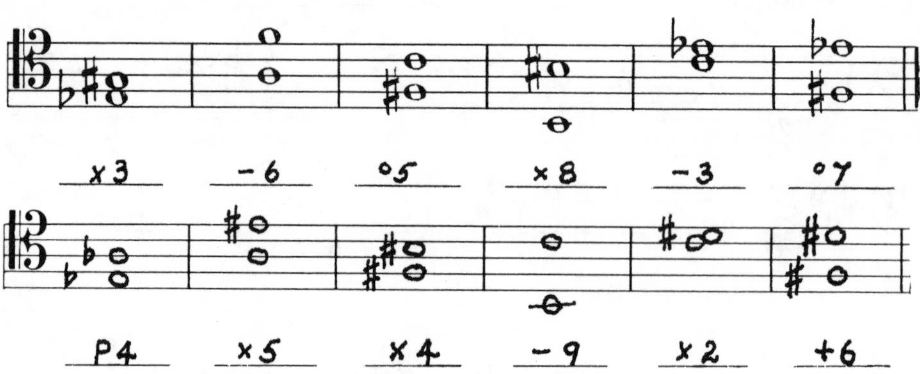

12 IV For each of the following dominant seventh chords give a) the root b) the position c) the key.

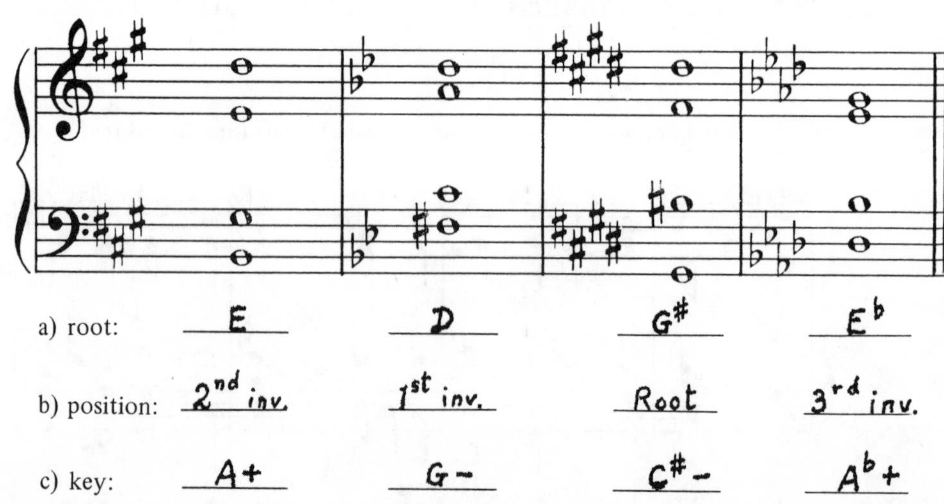

8 V Write a cadence at the end of each phrase of the following melody, and name each cadence.

10 VI Transpose the following melody up a major second, using the correct key signature and omitting any unnecessary accidentals.

12 VII Complete the following bars with rests.

18 VIII Write an example of each of the four different kinds of triads, using F as the lowest note for each. Name each triad, and name all the keys in which each may be found.

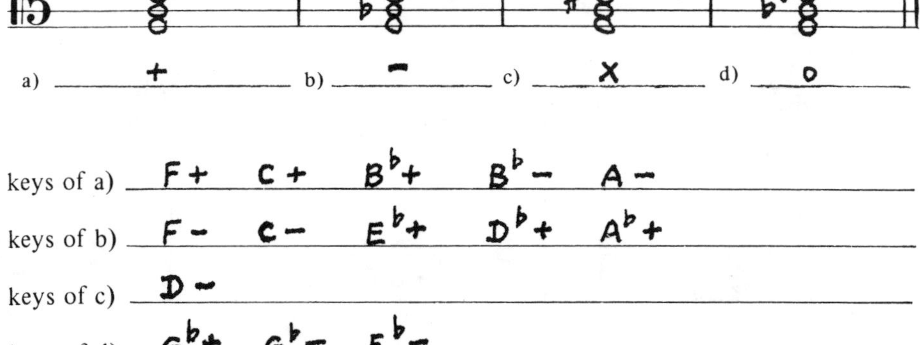

B C EXERCISES (to be done along with the exercises on pages 78 and 79.) (p. 200)

The following are the melody notes of either Perfect or Plagal Cadences. Complete them as shown above.

C EXERCISES (to be done after the exercises on page 82.) (p. 201)

The following are the melody notes of Perfect, Plagal or Imperfect Cadences. Complete them as shown above. *

* In some examples other keys and cadences are possible.